Housing Options for Independent Living Programs

Number 2 in a series of youth work resources

Mark J. Kroner

CWLA Press • Washington, DC

CWLA Press is an imprint of the Child Welfare League of America. The Child Welfare League of America (CWLA), the nation's oldest and largest membership-based child welfare organization, is committed to engaging all Americans in promoting the well-being of children and protecting every child from harm.

CHILD WELFARE LEAGUE OF AMERICA, INC.
440 First Street, NW, Third Floor, Washington, DC 20001-2085
E-mail: books@cwla.org

CURRENT PRINTING (last digit)
10 9 8 7 6 5 4 3 2 1

Cover design by Veronica J. Morrison

Printed in the United States of America

ISBN # 0–87868-752-1

Library of Congress Cataloging-in-Publication Data
Kroner, Mark.
    Housing options for independent living programs / Mark Kroner.
        p.   cm.
    ISBN 0-87868-752-1 (alk. paper)
    1. Youth--Services for--United States.   2. Youth--Housing--United
States.   3. Youth--United States--Life skills guides.   4. Group
homes for youth--United States.   I. Title.
HV1431.K76 1999   98-47846
362.7'083--dc21   CIP

When I was in the ILP, they made me do everything myself. I had to get on a bus to get groceries and carry two bags back to my place. I had to carry a basket of laundry down two blocks and back again—and I had to pay to get it done. I had to cook my own food, clean it all up, and if I forgot to empty the trash, it got pretty nasty. I couldn't blame being late on anybody else and if I spent my last dime on cigarettes, I had to walk three miles to get my next check. Yeah, independent living, they didn't do nothing for me. I did it all by myself.

Contents

Foreword

Each year in the United States, 25-35,000 young adults, ages 18 to 21, must leave the foster care system and take on all the responsibilities of adult life. Unlike their "mainstream" peers, most of these emancipating foster youth make the transition to self-sufficiency without the resources and supports that many young adults take for granted.

Until policymakers establish more realistic guidelines for services to older foster youth, we must rely on existing services that emphasize preparation for independence in real-life ways and in real-life settings. Independent living programs (ILPs) help young people acquire the knowledge, skills, and attitudes they will need to succeed, and one critical component of independent living is the setting in which these youth live.

Perhaps no one person in the field of youth services and independent living has contributed more to the discussion of the relationship between youth services and settings than Mark Kroner. For many years, Mark has divided his time between thinking about how best to implement independent living services and actually running an ILP. In *Housing Options for Independent Living Programs*, he emphasizes program structure and implementation in a variety of settings. The strategies that he offers are useful to any practitioner wishing to strengthen a program's capacity to prepare young people for the transition to adult-hood.

This second volume of the **Youthwork Resource Series** will assist those workers who are in the field helping youth make that transition (and supporting them when those transitions are not successful). The practical information offered in this volume is enhanced by its reliance on relevant anecdotal stories from youth workers who have consulted with the author.

I had the opportunity to participate in an independent living training conducted by Mark many years ago as I prepared to start up a scattered-site apartment program. His experience and wisdom, as well as his ability to clearly communicate what works and what doesn't, provided an effective, strengths-based foundation for our program.

The Child Welfare League of America is pleased to offer Mark's experience and wisdom to the field. We are confident that youth across the country will benefit from *Housing Options for Independent Living Programs*.

Robin Nixon, Director
CWLA Youth Development Program

Acknowledgments

I would like to thank Byron Wright of the Kenosha Human Services in Wisconsin for his help on this project. His insights and expertise from running his agency's independent living program for more than a decade were invaluable.

I would also like to thank Bob Mecum, Executive Director of Lighthouse Youth Services, for his leadership and "let's give it a try" attitude, and Jean Sepate, Assistant Executive Director of Lighthouse Youth Services, for her problem-solving skills.

Finally, I would like to thank Shahzaade Ali and the staff of the Lighthouse Independent Living Program for their endless efforts to help the youth in our program have a better chance at success in life.

Introduction

"But won't all of the girls get pregnant living by themselves?" *"Well, we once received five girls from a group home that closed and four of them were at least four months pregnant. And that was with double coverage in the evening and 24-hour-a-day staffing. These kids know more about birth control options than we ever did at their age. If a young woman wants to get pregnant, it probably will happen. But, I think our statistics would show that our ILP's pregnancy rate is about the same as the general population. Many of the girls in our program have had children before they were 17 and come into the program with them. We would like to help them realize that their lives would go more smoothly without a second child."*

This book is designed to help care providers decide on the best mix of living arrangement options and services for the youth in their care who cannot return home to live with their families. Since the Federal Independent Living Initiative was launched in 1986, many communities now have life skills training and other related services in place and are realizing that, without a place to stay and a chance to put life skills training to practice, youth will leave care in a very vulnerable position.

Part I of this book, Housing Options, provides a basic survey of many of the existing program models in operation today. Part II, Housing Issues, examines the challenges of operating independent living programs. Finally, Part III, The Future of Independent Living Programs, looks at how to measure the success of a program—and what these successes mean for the future.

I took over the Lighthouse Youth Services Independent Living Program in 1986, a few years after the program was started by Bob Mecum, the agency executive director, and a small group of adventuresome social workers. Then called New Life Youth Services, the agency really saw independent living services as an essential means of helping youth who couldn't return home exit from the system. The agency also recognized that the scattered-site model was worth the effort and would be the basis from which the program would grow.

Many gray hairs later, I still find myself excited by the challenges and believe more than ever that youth are benefiting greatly from their time in the Independent Living Program (ILP), based on what I (and others) see and what clients tell me (and others).

Most of the examples throughout the book are examples of strategies being tested in up-and-running programs around the country. I decided against providing the names of staff or agencies, because in my experience, by the time a book like this is published (and given today's rapidly changing environment), the people running the programs might have changed or the programs might have evolved into some other service variation. The resource people and organizations in Appendix A have all been involved in the field for a long time and hopefully will be for years to come. Most of them will be able to help you with questions or connect you with someone who can. I hope this helps you help the youth you serve!

Definitions

Here are working definitions for the terms used in this book. Some of the terms, e.g., "transitional living," mean something different to everyone using them. Your region might have a different term than the one used in this book.

- **Institution:** A large structured facility or group of facilities housing anywhere from 40 to several hundred youth with most services provided on-grounds.

- **Residential treatment center:** A facility or group of facilities usually serving between 15 to 40 youth and utilizing a combination of on-grounds and community-based services.

- **Community-based group home:** A house of six to 15 youth in the community, which uses existing community services, but also provides some treatment by around-the-clock trained staff.

- **Specialized family foster home:** A situation in which a youth is placed with a community family specially licensed to provide care and sometimes specifically trained to provide independent living services.

- **Shelter:** A facility whose purpose is to provide short-term emergency housing to teens in crisis.

- **Live-in roommate (mentor apartments):** A situation in which a youth shares an apartment with an adult or student who serves as a mentor or role model. The apartment can be rented or owned by either the adult or the agency.

- **Host home:** A situation in which a youth rents a room in a family or single adult's home, sharing basic facilities and agreeing to basic rules, while being largely responsible for his/her own life.

- **Boarding home:** A facility that provides individual rooms for youth or young adults, often with shared facilities and minimal supervisory expectations.

- **Shared house:** A minimally supervised house shared by several young adults who take full responsibility for the house and personal affairs. These homes may or may not have live-in staff.

- **Semi-supervised apartment** (scattered-site apartments): A privately owned apartment rented by an agency or youth in which a youth lives independently or with a roommate, with financial support, training, and some monitoring.

- **Supervised apartment:** An apartment building, rented or owned by an agency, in which numerous youth live with a live-in supervisor who occupies one of the units.

- **Single room occupancy:** A room for rent, often near a city center.

- **Specialized group home:** Sometimes also referred to as semi-independent living programs, these homes are usually staffed as a group home, but house older teens and focus on developing self-sufficiency skills.

- **Subsidy programs:** A situation in which a youth receives a monthly stipend that can be used toward a self-chosen living arrangement and food and personal supplies. The youth must follow certain agency guidelines.

- **Subsidized housing:** Government-supported, low-income housing. Monthly rent is based on income.

- **Transitional living group home*:** A home affiliated with a residential treatment center to which older teens move upon completing treatment goals.

- **Transitional living for older nonsystem youth*:** Any living arrangement supported by funds from federal grant funds for older nonsystems youth.

Factors That Drive the Need for Independent Living Services

- There are close to 500,000 children and youth in the foster care system nationwide, many of whom will not be able to return to their families[1].

- Many youth enter the child welfare system in their teen years and often do not want to be placed in a foster or group home. It is virtually impossible to find people willing to adopt troubled older teens.

- Welfare reform is making the need for self-sufficiency skills development vital to the very survival of youth who cannot live with their families.

- Nearly 22 million adult children live with one or both parents. Young adults from "normal" families are not able to move out on

---

*   Always ask what a person means when s/he uses the term "transitional living." It continues to have many meanings around the country.

their own due to the high cost of housing and difficulty finding jobs that pay enough[2].

- Many homeless adults were formerly in the foster care system and did not learn the skills needed to function responsibly in the community.

- Budget crises and managed care strategies lead to shortened stays in the system; there is an emphasis on low-cost, least-restrictive, community-based, step-down services.

- Youth making positive adjustments to supervised settings find it hard to adjust to situations where there are no adults to monitor their actions. Responsible care providers are feeling that it's best to give youth the chance to go through this trial-and-error period while still in care.

Ten Basic Assumptions

This book is based on some basic assumptions about the way youth (and people in general) learn and change. For some youth, these might not apply. Some youth arrive in a program with astounding strength and maturity. These youth want to learn and probably would make it anywhere. But most youth entering independent living programs are not thinking about the joys of paying utility bills on time! Listed below are the basic assumptions.

- **Teens learn only when they have to.** An ILP's job is to help a youth understand the "have to."

- **Teens learn best by doing.** All of the life skills classes in the world won't help without the direct experience of putting those skills to use in a realistic situation.

- **The development of internal motivation and controls is the #1 goal.** Our goal should be to help a teen get to the "I did this because it's good for me" stage of thinking.

- **Self-esteem comes from learning how to do things.** Actually, self-esteem comes from lot of sources, but let's assume that a lot of it comes from taking responsibility for yourself and completing tasks that help you survive and work toward a better future.

- **Action is more important than insight.** Some therapists might argue this point, but many youth are not readily seeking to explore the pain of recent losses and, given the unrealistic time frame we have to work with, it's probably better to focus on what things can be changed.

- **Teens must make mistakes and feel real-life consequences before they become responsible.**

- **The closer you are to the life style you will be leading when out of the system, the less traumatic your exit from the system will be.** Imagine leaving the system at 18 and then at the same time having to look for a place to live. Models that place a youth in a living arrangement where he or she can remain after discharge greatly diminish the anxiety of termination.

- **Separation anxiety can dissipate over time.** In the old days it was, "Well, now you're 18, where do you want me to take your stuff?" Hopefully, now a youth will have at least a year of training and experience related to functioning independently before being discharged from care.

- **Fundamental change can be accomplished by adding new behaviors on top of old ones.** We might not be able to change someone's basic habits, but maybe we can add some new positive behaviors—add enough and there isn't time for those old nasty habits!

- **This is not necessarily the ideal way for a youth to go out on his or her own.** It's the best we can do, given the youth's situation and the unrealistic time frame we have. Most American youth stay at home or return home from time to time after they leave, or they are partially or fully supported while in college.

A Sample Voice Mail Progress Report

Week 1. "He isn't doing anything, he lies a lot, his place is a mess and he's always asking for a ride."

Week 5. "He's not doing much, he lies a lot, but at least he's fixing his own meals. He looks okay."

Week 9. "He's still not doing much but he's living alone, fixing his own meals, getting himself to the office on the bus, and his place looks better."

Week 14. "He's doing a little more, he started back to school, he's getting there on his own, his place looks all right, and he seems to be eating well."

Week 19. "He's going to school, looking for a job, and his place looks good."

Week 30. "He's going to school, working part-time, and he looks great, but he still lies from time to time. His place is better than before—he's really doing a lot for himself if you think about it."

Why the Need for Alternative Living Arrangement Options?

Independent living options address some of the shortcomings of traditional options (foster care, group homes, residential treatment centers, etc.), which are listed below:

- They often promote dependency.

- They are usually more expensive.

- They do not always resemble the place where a youth would return or live after care.

- They can prevent the development of self-sufficiency skills.

- They are not always in the neighborhoods to which a youth returns.

- They focus on group control with many problems coming from the grouping of several or many high-risk youth.

- They focus on deficits and behaviors related to adjustment to the setting in which a youth lives.

- They often end at age 18 and require a move to a new living arrangement upon discharge.

- They do not always give firsthand experience in managing space, time, food preparation, laundry, money, etc.

Issues to Consider When Establishing Housing Options for Independent Living

Regardless of the type or mix of housing models that a community chooses to utilize, a number of issues must be considered in advance.

- **Community support/zoning issues:** Will the local community block attempts to establish or operate a supervised apartment program (Not In My Back Yard!)? Are there codes that would hinder the development of small group living arrangements or supervised apartment buildings? Would there be complaints about an ILP placing teens on their own? Would this be seen as too risky or even cruel to the youth?

- **Court support**: Does the local juvenile court support placement into a chosen living arrangement? Can the ILP obtain written court orders authorizing such placements? Do local judges, magistrates, and referees know the purpose of placing system youth in specific living arrangements?

- **Affordability**: Can the ILP afford to make rental payments in a chosen apartment? Can the client afford to pay the apartment rent after discharge? Can the ILP afford to lose deposit money either by turning the apartment over to the youth or losing the deposit due to damages and/or breaking the lease?

- **State licensing**: Does your state have codes that allow for less restrictive and semi-supervised models, such as scattered-site apartments?

- **Safety**: Is the choice of living arrangement in a relatively safe neighborhood? Could the tenants in the building cause problems for the ILP or the client? Is the property well-lit at night? Is there a locked security door to gain entrance into the building? Is the apartment in good condition? Do the windows lock? Can anyone easily get into the apartment (e.g., a basement apartment with windows that can't be locked)?

- **Accessibility**: Is the chosen apartment/living arrangement close to transportation options and near shopping areas and employment opportunities?

- **Long-term possibilities**: When the youth is discharged from care, can he/she keep the apartment and take over the lease and rental payments? Will the landlord consider this as a possibility? (If not, it might be worth looking longer for landlords who will allow this to happen.) If the program operates a multiunit supervised apartment situation, will the youth have to leave the building as soon as support payments stop?

- **Neighborhood/environment**: Is this neighborhood safe for a single youth? Will the neighbors/tenants be a negative factor in the youth's life? Will this arrangement tolerate the normal antics of a teen living alone (lots of visitors, constant music, late night TV, etc.)? It's worth taking some time and talking with neighbors and tenants about the realities of the neighborhood and apartment building or complex.

- **Organizational capability**: Does the ILP's agency have the funds necessary to advance money for deposits, rent, utilities, furnishings, supplies, moves, etc., before reimbursement payments arrive? Does the agency have staff available to be on call 24-hours-a-day, seven-days-a-week, 365-days-a-year? Does the agency board support the risk involved in less restrictive settings? Are there alternative placement options within the agency in case an arrangement doesn't work out?

- **Cultural fit**: Would this youth feel at home/safe in this neighborhood? In this building? On this street? Take care to place a youth in a neighborhood that fits his/her cultural background. Would the youth tend to spend more time in another neighborhood? Is there gang activity that might place this youth in jeopardy? Do staff feel comfortable placing a youth in this neighborhood? Would staff feel comfortable visiting a client on this street?

The Basics of a Comprehensive Independent Living Program

- **Awareness of need:** Care providers and administrators know the importance of preparing youth in out-of-home care to learn how to take responsibility for their survival after care.

- **All systems participating:** State officials, licensing staff, judges, referees, guardians ad litem, social workers, foster parents, group home staff, residential treatment center staff, etc., all take action to help teens learn self-sufficiency skills.

- **Life skills training:** A variety of opportunities exist to help youth learn life skills (early and often), weekly classes, weekend retreats, Saturday all-day workshops, self-guided workbooks, computer software, mentors, volunteers, students, etc.

- **Committed people:** A handful of people (or sometimes just one) who have the people skills, stamina, and persistence to stick around long enough to make something happen.

- **Positive connections:** To landlords, employers, counselors, schools, medical people, court personnel, local administrators, funders, etc.

- **Real-life experience:** A chance for youth to put skills to practice, make mistakes and learn from them, and adjust to the idea of taking full responsibility for their life.

- **Stable sources of funding:** Long-term contracts, grants, donations, gifts, bequests, etc.

- **Housing at termination:** A potential long-term, affordable place for a youth leaving care to stay, hopefully furnished with the basics.

- **Aftercare:** Opportunities to assist youth after they are discharged from care.

- **Linkages with the adult system of care** for youth who may have issues that will require ongoing case management for many years.

- **Rules and regulations** at the local and state levels that allow for the use of less restrictive living arrangement options.

The following section, Part I, Housing Options, describes the various housing options available for independent livings and provides examples of each.

Note: Throughout the text, I have provided examples of "Ongoing ILP Conversations" to illustrate situations that commonly arise when youth are learning to live on their own. These are indicated by *italic type.*

Notes

1   Child Welfare League of America. (1997). *State agency survey.* Cited in Petit, M. R., & Curtis, P. A. (1997). *Child abuse and neglect: A look at the states. 1997 CWLA stat book.* Washington, DC: CWLA Press.
2.   Bryson, K., & Casper, L. M. (1997). *Household and family characteristics: March 1997.* Washington, DC: U.S. Census Bureau.

Part I: Housing Options

1
Scattered-Site Apartments

"Boris, this rug looks like bad modern art! We'll take some money out of your savings to get it cleaned. But as we discussed, if it gets worse, you might have to pay to replace it when you leave; it was brand new when you moved in."

A scattered-site apartment is an individual apartment, usually rented from a private landlord, in which a youth is placed, usually alone, while in custody or care to experience living independently.

Examples

Example #1

Robert is in a foster home and recently celebrated his seventeenth birthday. The county has made numerous efforts to engage his mother, who has chronic mental health issues, and his aunt, who lives in the city. Neither of them feel they can help support him in any way because of their own problems. The county child services caseworker knows Robert will need to support himself not long after he is 18.

A referral is made to a local nonprofit organization that has established an ILP. That nonprofit interviews Robert and accepts him into their ILP. With Robert's participation, and a bit of salesmanship on the part of the nonprofit social worker, an apartment is located in the school district he attends. Since Robert is 17, the nonprofit signs the lease and keeps a copy of the key. Robert is informed that, since the apartment is in the nonprofit's name, he can be pulled out immediately if problems persist.

A moving date is set and the program staff pick up Robert several days ahead of the move to search the thrift shops for furnishings ("Don't you have any couches that aren't brown plaid?") and supplies ("I'm sorry, all of these towels have 'Hotel California' written on them.").

Example #2

Bill has been living in a treatment center for chemical dependency issues and has done well in the program. Under the custody of the juvenile court due to chronic delinquency and parental neglect, he is in need of independent living skills training because his parents are divorced, whereabouts unknown. The court refers Bill to a local nonprofit ILP, where he is interviewed for their scattered-site apartment program.

Bill does well at the interview, but the ILP is not sure he will be able to avoid a quick relapse back to his pretreatment state. The ILP negotiates a contract with Bill for him to get a chance in the program. He agrees to attend Alateen meetings daily for the first three weeks in the program, to call daily from his GED program, and to meet twice a week with a graduate student to work on life skills. He agrees to random drug screens to be completed by his probation officer, who also wants a daily phone call from Bill. He will also give the ILP $150 from his savings toward a deposit on his apartment. If he successfully completes the program, he will get his deposit back. If not, he loses it. Even though Bill will be living on his own, he has a structure and set of expectations that can help him adjust to this major change.

Example #3

Julie, 16, is in a youth shelter due to chronic sexual abuse by her mother's boyfriend. Child protection staff have convinced the court that Julie needs to be taken into custody, and the court agrees. Julie has been doing well in school and has a part-time job not far from her home. A local ILP is able to find a landlord who has a second floor of a house for rent. ILP staff move Julie's bed, dresser, and personal items into the apartment, which already has a stove and refrigerator.

After the apartment is furnished with the basics, Julie is given a key, as is her assigned social worker, a 24-hour emergency number, and is told to call the ILP office twice daily. The ILP social worker will visit her daily for the first week and then cut back, depending on her adjustment. Julie is able to stay in her school and keep her job, as the apartment is in the same part of town. The agency will cover her rent, utility, and phone bills until she is 17 1/2 , at which point she will start covering part of these bills. She will also receive $45 weekly to cover food, transportation, and personal items. Any clothing will have to be purchased with her work earnings.

Example #4

Jason has done well in the Washington Correctional Center and is ready for release. His mother is in a homeless shelter and his father's whereabouts are unknown. He is referred to an ILP in the city of his birth and after an interview, is scheduled to move into his own apartment.

ILP staff know that going from a highly structured setting to almost complete freedom is a big jump for Jason. With his input, a plan is made for him to attend daily GED classes, weekly individual counseling, weekly visits to his parole officer's office, and weekly visits to the ILP office. He is to start looking for a job and will wear an electronic monitoring bracelet to enforce a 9 P.M. curfew until he starts his job. ILP staff will make random, unannounced visits to his apartment.

Example #5

Shana has been to the local youth crisis shelter three times in the last month due to domestic violence on the part of her alcoholic father. The child protection worker was convinced that Shana's home situation was extremely dangerous and eventually she was taken into custody. Shana was mature for her age (16), and a B student with a steady job. She served as the family caretaker and was often the acting parent in the household. Shana felt uncomfortable about going to a foster home and all involved felt that she could handle living alone.

She was referred to the county's ILP and told to start looking for an apartment. She contacted several landlords and explained the program, stating that the program would sign the lease, pay the deposit, and help her with rent, utilities, and phone bills. The landlord called the ILP office to get the facts and was sent a copy of the program description, the client policy manual, and the 24-hour emergency number.

The landlord agreed to give her a try. Shana moved into an apartment near her job and school. If she continues to do well and finds a full-time job after she graduates, she will be able to take over the apartment and all its furnishings, leaving the system with a fully furnished place to live and many months of experience living alone. She will have made the emotional adjustments to her new reality and can begin the process of making peace with her troubled family, while not depending on them.

Advantages

Listed below are the basic assumptions underlying a scattered-site apartment program model:

- Youth (people) learn best by doing, when feeling the consequences of their actions directly (within reason, of course).

- Youth learn best when they have no other choice, when they have to take action on their own behalf. All of the classes and training in the world do not have the impact of a month living alone in an apartment, feeling the responsibility for time management, apartment management, shopping, food preparation, etc.

- An organization does not have to purchase and maintain a piece of property. Clients can be accepted immediately if apartments can be located with landlords willing to rent to teens.

- The clients can choose a location that is convenient for them, close to work, school, and social support network.

- The clients can keep the apartment, the furnishings, and the security deposit, and leave the system with a fully furnished living arrangement with long-term possibilities.

- The size of the program is not limited to the amount of agency-owned apartment units.

- Group and crowd control problems are not the primary issue. Most problems reported by supervised apartment programs are due to interactive problems between residents. In some cases, they are like group homes with less supervision.

- In an independent apartment, a youth is forced to develop an internal locus of control—to realize that his/her actions must be self-supervised and not due to the presence of a caregiver or enforcer.

- The transition to self-reliant living will be smoother if the living arrangement resembles the future situation of the youth. The jump from a program with an abundance of resources, staff, and other people to life alone can be unsettling and confusing.

- The youth must develop coping skills to deal with loneliness, control of visitors, and the skills to deal with fellow tenants, landlords, etc., from which s/he is protected in a supervised setting.

- The scattered-site model is an ideal public/private partnership, with community landlords receiving a large portion of the program's budget and available housing being utilized fully. It makes the best use of available housing resources.

- For many of the young adults who enter the system or are otherwise without a true home, their central issue is having some type of control over their lives. Giving a youth a personal space is perhaps the most significant form of empowerment.

- Many landlords are also "ad hoc social workers." They reinforce many expectations necessary for successful apartment living in a much more realistic method.

In sum, the scattered-site model is close to a real-life situation, future-oriented, and a move away from the time- and capital-consuming idea of finding and developing of new properties.

Disadvantages

- This is a risky business, even at best. Youth can cause problems for other tenants, cause damages to the property, and do other things that can cost money and public relations problems. Boards can hinder program development due to liability concerns. Local juvenile court and children service staff might not feel comfortable with the risks involved.

- Friends and relatives of the client can cause problems and damages or could actually take over the place and create safety issues for program staff.

- No one knows how a youth will adapt to living alone. Some youth do not have the prerequisite common sense or judgment to live alone without causing daily problems. Finding this out can be a less than positive experience for the ILP, landlord, other tenants, and community.

- Some communities lack affordable or available apartments. Available apartments might not be close to public transportation or employment opportunities.

- A scattered-site program needs to be staffed by experienced social workers who have a "sixth sense" to ward off problems before they get out of hand. These staff also need to be able to sleep without worrying about all of the things that really could go wrong.

- This model is not always the best first choice for chemically dependent youth, youth with recent suicide attempts or severe depressions, or youth with chronic criminal activities or chronic mental health issues. However, some of these high-risk youth do better alone than in group settings.

- Loneliness can cause some youth to stray from the program's goals and violate the rules by having endless gatherings of friends or over night visitors.

Other Observations

- Some programs have found landlords that will let a minor youth sign a lease, without a program co-signer. This limits the liability of the organization.

- Clients must have some basic maturity and common sense to make it in this model.

- Finding willing landlords can be difficult at first, but gets easier after you've had several successes and can use previous landlords as a reference.

- Logistical issues are endless—not unlike a chess game being played in a storm!

- Minimizing empty apartments is important to keep losses down.

- In many ways, the bigger a scattered-site program gets, the easier it is run. Open apartments can quickly be utilized by new clients or clients getting a second chance. But staff must be able to keep track of hundreds of details and sense and head off possible problems.

 "Mr. Rogers, we're sorry for the disturbance last night. We have a policy against baby showers in our program apartments and our client broke it. We never knew she had such an extended family. Those buses sure made a mess of parking in your neighborhood last night. We're really sorry, and we'll make sure it won't happen again. Here's our 24-hour crisis line—call it and one of us will be here ASAP."

"William, you should have asked the landlord before using black light paint on your ceiling. You'll have to pay to have it repainted. By the way, you misspelled Hendrix."

2
Supervised Apartments

ILP social worker Ann was shocked to see the huge new entertainment system in Jerry's new apartment.
"Where did you get this, Jerry?" asked Ann.
"From Jake's Rent-to-Own Center last night. They delivered it and set up too!"
"But, you're only 17!" said Ann.
"Yeah, but what they don't know, won't hurt me," replied Jerry.

A supervised apartment building is usually owned by an agency that houses youth in separate apartments and is supervised by live-in or overnight staff.

Examples

Example #1

Steve is 16 and relatively mature. He will not be able to live with his mother when he is terminated from care, and he has no relatives who are willing to take him in. His foster parents feel that he needs experience living more independently before he turns 18. He is referred to a local program that owns a five-unit building. One of the units is occupied by a resident manager who has a full-time job but spends nights at the building.

Steve moves into the building and shares one of the apartments with a 17-year-old student. The other three apartments also have roommate pairs. Steve has a curfew and is assigned chores, but is pretty much on his own. He attends a life skills group on Saturday mornings and an all-house meeting on Sunday nights, during which both progress and conflicts are discussed.

Example #2

Cain has been in a residential treatment center for the last year. His progress is sporadic, with periods of cooperation followed by periods of intense resistance. Although Cain hasn't "earned" his right to move into the agency's supervised independent living apartment program, his caseworker feels that he needs to be in a less restrictive living arrangement where she can see how well his view of the world works and where he can learn more from the consequences of his actions.

Cain moves in an apartment on the second floor with his new roommate Abel. There are a total of eight clients in the building, which is owned by the agency. For a few days they get along, but then tensions arise from Abel's problem with Cain's hygiene. The resident manager, who lives in the basement apartment, has to set up almost daily meetings to get the two to stop their squabbling. The resident manager writes up the terms of a "truce" in which Cain promises to keep himself and his area cleaner and Abel promises to be less of a perfectionist. As time goes by, there are still problems, but the two roommates seem to be doing more things together and have actually talked of eventually moving into their own apartment when discharged.

Example #3

Sally is 17 and really has done well in her foster home. But she and her foster parents know that she needs to get ready for the next step. The foster care program is affiliated with a supervised apartment program in the community. The agency purchased an old strip motel on the major road running through town. It has ten units and an office building. This "semi-independent living" program is for females only. A program director/resident manager lives in the office building and two other youth workers spend time at the office during the day. Each unit is equipped with a refrigerator, hot plate, and microwave—a makeshift efficiency kitchen.

Sally moves into one of the units and meets with her assigned youth worker every evening after school. She really doesn't have a lot of time to hang out with the other girls in the motel, due to school and work schedules. She especially avoids Evella in the third unit whom everyone knows is using drugs and trying to sneak in guys. Sally will live in this situation until she graduates from high school and then will be assisted in finding her own place. Her foster parents have her over for dinner every Sunday.

Advantages

- Agencies often can acquire a building for little or no money and might be able to get funding for rehab costs. HUD funds and city housing funds are often sources of financial support.

- Group counseling and/or life skills training can be easier to organize with all clients in one place.

- Youth can learn daily from the mistakes of others.

- One competent and charismatic resident manger with leadership skills can develop a positive peer atmosphere that can be effective.

- A positive peer environment can magnify the direction of agency staff and pressure all residents to do well.

- Youth can assume almost all responsibilities.

- The arrangement recognizes that many youth still need daily attention and supervision.

Disadvantages

- Group and crowd control issues can occur. One negative client can interrupt or disturb the progress of all other residents

- If it's an all-female program, uninvited males can be a constant problem.

- If it's an all-male problem, groups of visiting friends and under-age girls can be a problem.

- The agency usually has to purchase a building, rehab it, and go through a lengthy licensing and/or zoning process.

- The "Not in My Back Yard" issue can slow down or block the development of any group living program.

- Once a youth is discharged from the system, s/he usually has to leave the apartment building and find another place to stay.

- All clients must live in the same part of town and might have to attend school in the district.

- The success of this model often depends on the qualities and motivation of the resident manager and support staff. It can be more of a lifestyle than a job. Turnover can be a problem.

- If the program needs to be licensed as a group home, the agency might be required to have costly coverage staff.

- Expenses for this model remain constant regardless of the number of residents.

Other Observations

- Can provide a more realistic independent living experience than a foster or group home.

"Alphonso, there are only two windows left in this complex. I like your music, but these six-foot super-woofers are bringing the house down. Alphonso, can you hear a word I'm saying? Alphonso....!"

"Hank, we discussed your responsibility for controlling the thermostat in your apartment. Your bill for February was $125! As we discussed at orientation, we only budget $40 a month. Apparently, you kept the temperature set at 90 de-grees, even when you weren't here. You'll have to help us out with this. We're going to take $5 a week out of your allowance."

3
Shared Homes

 "The bottom shelf is my food, the top is Steve's, and the middle one's yours. If Steve loses his job, you're better off eating out somewhere, 'cause he'll clean you out foster than the speed of light."

A shared home is a minimally supervised house shared by several young adults who take full responsibility for the house and personal affairs. Shared homes may or may not have live-in adults.

Examples

Example #1

Carl is 17 and has been in a foster home for the last five years. He is developmentally disabled with an IQ of 64. He has a lot of common sense, gets along well with adults, and knows when he needs to ask for help. However, his caseworker doesn't feel comfortable moving him directly to his own apartment, and he refuses to go to a group home for older teens. A local agency operates a small home that has three beds for males 16 to 19 and a staff member who lives on the first floor of the house. Two youth share one bedroom and one has his own room.

Everyone shares the kitchen, but the resident manager has his own bathroom. Carl visits the home and decides he want to give this a try. The plan is for Carl to live in the shared home for three months to assess his level of independent functioning. The resident manager will report Carl's progress and ability to take care of himself in the "semi-independent living" situation. If all goes well, Carl will leave the system after living three to six more months in his own apartment.

Example #2

Sheila was placed in her own apartment last month and has had nothing but trouble. She can't seem to limit or control her friends and has consistently missed her curfew. After several unheeded warnings, ILP staff decided to move her out of her apartment. The ILP also operated a shared-home in another part of town and a bed was open. Staff went to her apartment and helped her pack her things. Sheila was angry and couldn't believe that ILP staff really followed through on their warning. Sheila did agree to follow a contract that would give her another chance to have her own apartment in one month if she acted more responsibly and met the terms of the contract.

Example #3

ILP client Erin lived in her own apartment for several months and was doing quite well. While biking on the weekend, she broke her leg in a bad fall. ILP staff moved her into a shared home with two other female clients. She stayed at the home for three weeks, until she was able to get around a little better on her own, then she moved back to her own apartment.

Advantages

- Live-in staff have daily contact with clients.
- Usually no need to go through zoning or licensing process.
- House might be available from HUD or local government.
- Funds for rehabbing a building might be available locally or federally.
- Can be more cost-effective than scattered sites, especially if the building is free.

- Can be blended into a neighborhood more easily than a group home.

Disadvantages

- Client must leave the home and find a new place after discharge from care.
- This model's "workability" can depend on the personality and dedication of the resident manager.
- Resident manager burnout and turnover can be an issue.
- An all-girls shared home can attract unwanted male visitors.
- Agency has to find an available house and possibly sink a fair amount of money in fixing it up.
- Neighbors might not be happy.
- One bad apple ...
- A lot of time will be spent "refereeing" complaints among house-mates.

Other Observations

- Some agencies have tried shared homes without live-in adults—not unlike a group of college students living near campus.
- The success of this model depends on the mix and maturity of the residents.
- College students make good candidates for resident managers, especially if the house is near the campus.
- Plan on a yearly turnover of resident managers.

4

Live-in Adult/Peer Roommate Apartments

"Jill, your phone bill was $200! You apparently must like this guy in Alaska. But as we discussed, we cover only the basic $30 monthly bill. Your choice: do you want to pay us the balance out of your savings or do you want us to take it out gradually from your allowance? We put a long-distance block on your phone yesterday."

Live-in adult/peer roommate (or *mentor*) apartments provide a situation in which a youth shares an apartment with an adult or student who serves as a mentor or role model. The apartment can be rented or owned by either the adult or the agency.

Examples

Example #1

Tom is 16 1/2 and is limited in his ability to make good decisions on his own. His caseworker knows that Tom will never be able to live with his biological parents, both of whom can barely take care of themselves. Tom is referred to a local nonprofit ILP, which suggests that Tom live with an adult roommate instead of living by himself. The agency finds a graduate student who is willing to give this arrangement a try. The student, age 26, completes a screening and orientation process and is trained as a mentor/big brother/teacher.

The student will live rent-free in a two-bedroom apartment and will not have to pay utility or phone bills. Tom moves into the second bedroom and the two share cleaning chores. The student goes about his life and studies but is required to report daily on Tom's activities, attitude, and progress. The student reports any problems to the ILP social worker, who addresses them with Tom during weekly visits to the apartment.

The ILP also pays the grad student a small stipend to guide Tom through a life skills training program. Just by being around the student, Tom picks up hints on cooking, shopping, time management, bill paying, and apartment maintenance. The student will help Tom's caseworker and ILP social worker assess Tom's potential for eventually live on his own.

Example #2

Tina is 17 and recently discharged from an adolescent chemical dependency program. Tina's mom is a crack addict whose whereabouts are unknown, and her father moved away five years ago. Tina's caseworker does not feel that Tina is ready to have her own place, but she also knows that Tina really doesn't want to live in a foster or group home. Tina's caseworker contacts the local ILP and asks if they can come up with a creative solution to help prepare Tina for life after the child welfare system.

An advertising, interviewing, and screening process finds a 35-year-old single woman whose roommate recently moved out of their two-bedroom apartment. The woman is interviewed by the caseworker and ILP staff and completes a police check and a 12-hour orientation with the ILP. The woman has a full-time job but has contact with Tina in the evenings and weekends, especially when they fix meals together. The ILP receives an extra $10 a day from the custodial agency to cover the extra rent for the two-bedroom apartment and to give a small stipend to the roommate, who also has the ILP cover her rent.

Example #3

Tonya is 17 and living in a foster home. Although she is far from being ready to live on her own, everyone feels she needs to start getting some experience in independent living skills. Nobody, however, feels that she should be living alone at this point. A local ILP is willing to try a creative arrangement. The ILP has a former client who has a full-time job and is completely self-sufficient. This client has asked time and again to be able to teach new clients what she learned while she was in the ILP. This young woman is willing to take on the role of a live-in mentor. After all involved parties meet, the former client and Tonya feel comfortable giving it a try, the ILP rents a two-bedroom apartment for the client and mentor.

The mentor completes an orientation/training, and is told to think of herself as a big sister/guide, rather than a parent or authority figure. They both have rooms they can lock and decide to keep food and phones separate. The ILP pays the mentor's rent and gives her a small stipend. The mentor calls in several times a week to report on her contacts with Tonya. Tonya knows that if she does well in this situation, she will eventually get her own place.

Advantages

- An on-site mentor can be a continuous positive role model for a youth.
- High-risk youth (pregnant girls and chemically dependent or developmentally or physically disabled youth) could benefit from daily contact with a responsible person.
- The loneliness issue of the scattered-site model can be eliminated.
- A mentor with a car might be able to transport youth to school, work, or appointments.
- IL staff do not have to make as many site visits.
- Some communities and/or agency boards might want to try this model instead of having clients live alone.
- Local colleges might be able to supply students interested in the human services fields who want this type of experience.
- Some mentors go beyond expectations in helping a youth roommate prepare for the future.

- Open choice of location.

- Mentors can provide IL staff with daily observations and feedback.

Disadvantages

- The maturity level of the mentor might not be sufficient.

- A young adult mentor might quickly change life plans and need to move out.

- Youth set on living alone can sabotage the relationship.

- Dishonest youth can steal items from the mentor.

- Stylistic differences, e.g., music, food, friends, sleeping patterns, etc., can create daily tension.

- Allegations of any type of abuse could happen, due to the daily contact.

- Screening out people of questionable character and motivation is an issue.

- Mentors will probably need ongoing training and supervision.

- Abuse of the mentor by the youth could occur.

5

Specialized Foster Homes

 "Tanisha, honey, I know you're trying to learn how to cook. But we spent a lot of money redoing our kitchen and you're gonna burn the house down using all of that grease! That smoke alarm has been ringing for ten minutes. You should take off your headphones when you cook!"

Specialized foster homes are homes where a youth is placed with a community family specially prepared to provide training in independent living skills. Youth might exit the system from these situations and go directly to their own place without further community support.

Examples

Example #1

Zach is 17 and lives in a community without an established independent living program. His social worker and foster parents know that he will not be able to return to his family, as his father's whereabouts are unknown and his mom will be in prison for five more years. His foster parents have been specially trained to teach him self-sufficiency and independent living skills. Zach is learning how to cook, wakes himself up in the morning, and pays a token amount to the family to help them cover bills, and he is learning how to plan the use of his money. When Zach turns 18, the foster family will help get him set up in his own apartment. Even though he will no longer will be able to live with them, they will have lots of contact with him and help him when he runs into trouble.

Example #2

Stella is 17 and will be discharged on her eighteenth birthday, due to county budget cuts. She lives with a great foster family who have had her in their home since she was 10. Her father is deceased and her mom is severely mentally ill and is in and out of local hospitals on a regular basis. The foster family recently informed the county that Stella can live in their home after discharge from care. She will pay $100 a month toward her room and board, which she can easily afford with income from her savings and current job.

Example #3

LeAnn is 17 and will be discharged from foster care three months after she graduates in June. Her foster parents know she can't return to her biological family, due to issues of sexual abuse. Her foster parents actively teach her self-sufficiency skills using their own experience and a workbook given to them by the county. LeAnn also attends independent living classes on Saturday afternoons, where she meets other youth in her situation and learns from young adults who graduated from a local ILP and are now on their own. When LeAnn graduates from high school she will be referred to the foster care agency's ILP and placed in a scattered-site apartment. She will still have contact with her foster parents, but the goal is for her to take over the lease for the apartment shortly after she finds a full-time job.

Advantages

- Foster parents can be the best teachers and can give a youth daily lessons in self-sufficiency skills through modeling and teaching.

- Foster homes can include their own teens who, if mature, can yield positive influence on the foster teen.

- Foster parents might be part of the same agency that has an ILP program and can facilitate connections.

- Some foster parents let their foster youth remain living with them after discharge.

- Youth can leave foster homes with a sense that adults took an active part in their coming of age.

- Foster parents often raise numerous teens and have the wisdom from that experience to share with their current teen.

- Foster parents sometimes provide support for a youth for a life-time. The youth is seen as a member of the family.

- Foster homes can provide all of the benefits of family life.

- No size limit for referrals; not necessarily geographically fixed.

Disadvantages

- Foster parents might not want to focus on the youth's life after s/he leaves the foster home. This can promote dependency.

- Foster parents might be too restrictive and not allow a youth the opportunity to practice IL skills. Many foster parents have trouble allowing a youth to cook on her or his own or use the family's laundry machines.

- Foster parents who are having problems with their own youth might not be in a good position to assist another troubled teen.

- The foster home is usually not the place where the youth will live after discharge from care.

- The cultural and stylistic fit between the foster parents and youth might not match, creating daily battles concerning expectations of freedom and responsibility.

- An agency might not have foster families willing to take in older teens.

How Foster Parents Can Help Increase Self-Sufficiency

- Present a good example of responsible living.

- Be a model of communication and social skills.

- Provide opportunities to make decisions.

- Provide opportunities to manage/mismanage own time.

- Provide opportunities to manage/mismanage own money.

- Provide opportunities to learn how to shop and prepare food.

- Provide opportunities to talk about the future.

- Provide help in making realistic plans for the future.

- Provide help in learning how to shop for and prepare healthy meals.

- Teach them how to do laundry and care for clothing.

- Provide help in working through a life skills workbook.

- Provide help in develop healthy boundaries and relationships.

Other Observations

- Some youth find the intimacy provided by a foster home intimidating.

6

Host Homes

"Jill, I know you're getting terminated from county care at the end of the summer. You've been in our home for more than a year now, and we really enjoy your company. Why don't you think about staying here for a while? We'd ask you to kick in on room and board, but not half as much as you would pay for your own apartment."

A host home is where a youth rents a room in a family or single adult's home, sharing basic facilities and agreeing to basic rules while being largely responsible for his/her own life.

Host homes are similar to foster homes, except the host is not necessarily a licensed foster parent and does not usually have to go through the process of having the home licensed and the parent trained.

There are thousands of former foster parents in the country who either took a break from raising kids or became tired of the requirements of "the system," but who might be willing to once again open their homes up to older teens getting ready to go out on their own. A youth might identify a potential host through his/her own connections.

Youth in these situations are more free than foster youth to come and go as they please and are expected to manage time, money, school, work, and appointments without oversight from the host parent.

Host homes are a great solution in rural areas where apartment buildings are not available and house rentals are too expensive. The key to a successful host home placement is the fit between the host and the youth, as well as clear expectations, before placement, about the responsibilities of all parties. (See Appendix B for a sample of a host home contract.)

Examples

Example #1

Ron is 17 and everyone feels he is ready to leave the residential treatment center he has been at for the last year. He was removed from his family because of his sexual abuse of his sister and he can't go back home. No one feels comfortable placing Ron in his own apartment at first, although his caseworker and others feel he could handle the responsibility.

A former foster mother whose own children have all left offers to take Ron in as a boarder, as long as he agrees to some basic conditions, such as a curfew and respect for her property and possessions. Ron signs a contract created by his county caseworker, his host, and the nonprofit agency that has agreed to oversee the placement. The nonprofit will pay the host a monthly fee and cover half of the phone and utility bills.

Ron will stay with his host, attend sex-offender groups, and meet weekly with his program social worker. If he meets the terms of his contract, he will have the opportunity to remain living with his host until he can afford his own place.

Example #2

Diane is 17 and living in a foster home in a rural area. She is doing well at the local school and has a job at a local restaurant. Her child services caseworker knows that she will be cut off from county care on her eighteenth birthday and will not be able to return to her mom, who has serious mental health problems. There are no apartment buildings in this area, but the caseworker knows of a couple who expressed interest in helping the county with high-risk teens, but who didn't want to be foster parents. The couple had an extra bedroom open up when their daughter went away to college.

The caseworker worked out an arrangement where the couple would take Diane in as a boarder until she turned 18 and a private, nonprofit ILP in the next county would contract to supervise Diane and teach her independent living skills. The nonprofit would pay the couple $250 a month, as well as a portion of the phone and utility bills. The couple already had all furnishings and supplies covered and didn't want a security deposit. Diane would receive a weekly stipend from the ILP to cover food and personal items. The home would not need to be licensed as a foster home, and the couple would not serve an authoritative role with Diane.

Diane lived with the couple until she graduated from high school. At that point, Diane found a full-time job in the area. The couple asked Diane if she wanted to live with them for a while after she was discharged from care. Diane would be asked to kick in $125 a month and would still buy her own food. Diane was relieved not to have to move again and live by herself. She also didn't want to move into the city

Example #3

Frank lives in a rural area in a foster home with three other younger foster siblings. His caseworker feels he needs experience living on his own before he is discharged from care when he graduates from vocational school. He is really doing well in school and has a job at a gas station in town. The county has no independent living program and the county child services director doesn't want to start one, because he feels the county should not have to worry about a youth once he or she reaches 18.

This caseworker is a tireless advocate for the youth. She convinces the director and the local juvenile court judge to allow her to try a creative solution to this youth's problem. She finds an ILP in a neighboring county, which runs a scattered-site apartment program, to take on the case. The ILP soon finds out that there are virtually no available or affordable apartments to be rented in this county. The program places an announcement in several local church bulletins seeking someone to take this client in as a "boarder."

Several people inquire, and after numerous phone calls and interviews, the youth is placed in the home of a retired school teacher whose own kids are in college. Frank has his own room and is pretty much allowed to make himself at home. His host has to help him do a better job at cleaning up the kitchen after dinner and reminds him often to not mix darks and lights in the washer. Frank even starts liking his host's collection of surf music from the sixties and is surprised that his host cranks it up louder than he does!

Example #4

Annette is a 17-year-old who has a history of being sexually abused by her stepfather. While she was in group care, she experienced further sexual abuse and is now unwilling to live in any placement. She is intelligent and can graduate from high school if she can find a place to live. She is currently in a shelter.

She is referred to an ILP and an assessment is made that she is capable of living alone. When asked where she might want to live, she mentions a family she met through her church. The IL worker has her set up a meeting with the family, her county social worker, and ILP staff.

The family is receptive to the idea, as long as she continues to attend church and follow their rules. Annette moves in and the ILP subsidizes her rent and meets with the family twice monthly. Annette stays for 10 months, graduates from high school, and leaves to go to college.

Advantages

- No geographical limits.
- Families that provide housing can be quite supportive.
- Can work in rural areas where there are no apartment buildings or single room occupancies.
- A competent host could profoundly affect a youth's life.

- It's the old-fashioned way a community used to take care of its orphans.

- No need to sign a lease.

- Youth may find a family they know and who know what to expect from the youth. Host family can be a family of a friend, former foster parents, neighbors, friends of the family, etc.

- Provides daily adult contact and feedback to IL staff.

- Some hosts allow a youth to live with them after discharge from care.

Disadvantages

- If host has problems or is not a good role model, then youth can suffer.

- Potential for chronic relationship problems or allegations of abuse.

- A delinquent youth could steal from host or damage property.

- Host families can have unrealistic expectations about how well the youth will behave and will have little experience with "system" youth.

- Compatibility issues and a "values fit" are important.

Other Observations

- Some communities are concerned about potential problems or insufficient screening and training of hosts.

- Host family or adults need to have clear expectations about the arrangement and an understanding of potential problematic youth behaviors.

- Agencies should expect to provide support for the host family and continue to make regular visits to the home.

7
Boarding Homes

 "George, we want to respect your privacy, but if you get caught sneaking your girlfriend in at night, you'll have to go. Come on, guy, everybody can hear the fire escape going down in the middle of the night!"

A boarding home is a facility that provides individual rooms for youth or young adults, often with shared facilities and minimal supervisory expectations. This facility can be a YMCA or any similar single room occupancy (SRO) situation or a house opened to one or more boarders.

Examples

Example #1

Sandy is living in a group home and is doing well, but her caseworker feels she has maximized her learning from the home and needs to experience living independently to be ready to provide for herself when discharged from care. She is referred to a local ILP who sets up an interview date. At the interview, Sandy announces that she is three months pregnant, to the surprise of her caseworker and group home youth worker. Her care providers no longer feel comfortable with the idea of Sandy living alone, as she was vulnerable enough without the pregnancy. The ILP had a relationship with a local boarding home for women near the city center. The home was staffed 24 hours a day and had rooms for more than 150 women.

The boarding house would only allow a 17-year-old to move in be-cause of the ILP's track record of monitoring its clients. Julie would have her own room, but would have to share bathroom facilities. Julie resisted the idea but was told that if she followed program and board-ing home rules, kept her prenatal clinic appointments, met her curfew, and took good care of herself, then she would be assisted in finding her own apartment, hopefully at least a month before the baby was due. The home staff would call the ILP whenever Julie missed curfew or didn't return. The ILP would pay the boarding home $300 a month for Julie's room, but would not have to pay utilities or phone bills. If Julie proved unable to keep her part of the deal, then the ILP saved the time and money that they would have spent on setting Julie up in her own place.

Example #2

Marty is getting ready to leave the system. He wants to do things his own way and only has five months until he's 18. His foster parents know him well and have done the best they could to prepare him for life on his own. Marty has a job but only makes $100 a week. His fos-ter father tells him about a local recreation club that has a floor it rents out to adult males. The rooms go for $55 a week. He would have to eat at local restaurants, since there wasn't a cafeteria or kitchen, but he did that already. Marty already had enough saved for the deposit of $50. He wouldn't have to pay for utilities and could use a pay phone when he needed to make a call. Marty slept better knowing there was a place out there he could afford. He wouldn't stay there forever—just long enough to buy that houseboat he's been dreaming about.

Example #3

William (17 1/2-years-old) lives about 60 miles north of a county with an IL program. He spent most of his adolescence in residential treat-ment centers and was in the custody of his grandparents. He recently returned to their home and burglarized their house. He is sitting in the juvenile shelter with no potential placement. He also has Tourette's syndrome.

The county social worker contacts the ILP for a potential placement. The ILP director interviews William and accepts him for a placement in a local YMCA. William accepts the placement and after two months is arrested for attempted armed robbery. While in the program, he attended school, made most of his appointments, and was not employed.

This ILP was able to give William a chance, due to the availability of a program with a single rooms and great experience in dealing with difficult youth. The reason William was offered this opportunity had little to do with the likelihood of success, but it was simply his last, best, available option. SROs give a program the ability to give troubled youth with previous failed placements one more chance.

Example #4

Derek is a 17-year-old with six months until his eighteenth birthday. He has no criminal record but has no family willing to provide him a place to live. His father is unknown and his mother is homeless. Derek is struggling with defining his sexual identity. He is gay, a "cross-dresser" and wants to have a sex change operation. He has bouts of severe depression.

After considerable thought, the IL program decides to place him in the local YMCA. An extensive amount of preventive teaching is done with the YMCA staff about Derek's "different" behaviors. He completes high school, works occasionally, and faithfully makes all of his appointments. The ILP helps him get Social Security disability because of his inability to work (due to severe depression). He leaves the program voluntarily and moves to California where he plans to get a sex change operation.

Derek's stay in the ILP was deemed successful. He was allowed the freedom to be himself and the comfort of a living arrangement he could manage. The issues of depression were lessened somewhat by positive contacts with ILP staff and YMCA workers. The YMCA staff were also able to provide feedback to ILP staff, which would not have been possible in an individual apartment.

Advantages

- Can be accessed quickly.
- Might take difficult youth for short periods of time.
- Can be used as a back-up plan for youth who can't handle living alone or get evicted.
- Might be able to be rented weekly or daily.
- Can have staff who are supportive and good role models.
- Might not have to sign a lease
- Often have staff around the clock—more supervision than an individual apartment.
- Youth does need as high a maturity level as in an apartment.
- Might have recreational facilities (e.g., YMCAs).
- Can be an affordable long-term place for a youth to stay.
- Less potential for parties, drug use, criminal activities.

Disadvantages

- Mix of other boarders might be a problem.
- Might not be in best part of town.
- Might only take in youth older than 18
- Clients might come in contact with irresponsible youth or adults.
- Can bring clients into contact with predatory adults.
- The operators might be too lenient or might wait until things explode and then refuse to take any more of your agency's clients.

Other Observations

- Many buildings with SROs were torn down in the '80s and replaced with 30-story office buildings, many of which are often vacant. ("Maybe we could talk to the owners and turn one of the floors into ...")

- Many YMCA/YWCAs have low-cost housing for youth over the age of 18. Some agencies move youth into these situations when they turn 18.

- A key to success is being immediately responsive to complaints and providing lots of IL staff contact, and not depending on the boarding home staff to know everything going on with the youth.

- If things aren't working out, it might be better to pull the youth out quickly. It's better to lose a single placement than a long-term housing resource.

 "You're right, this is certainly a tough way to prepare a kid who has to take care of himself at such a young age, but we don't have the luxury of keeping him until he's ready. He'll be totally on his own in three months unless, of course, you can give us some more funding."

8

Transitional Group Homes

 "All right, some of you have been tossing out the dirty dishes on your chore night. We're switching to paper plates and chop sticks from here on out. And you're all on 8 P.M. curfew until we find out who took that case of Oreos from the pantry."

Transitional group homes are affiliated with a residential treatment center (RTC) or a community agency to which older teens move upon completing treatment goals

Examples

Example #1

Laura has spent the last six months in an RTC and has matured considerably. The RTC staff feel that she has met all of her treatment goals and is ready to move on. They also know that her mother refuses to leave the man who sexually abused Laura for years.

In state custody, Laura has no relatives able to support her and she made it clear she doesn't want to live in a foster home during her last seven months before she turns 18 and leaves care. The RTC has on its campus a transitional group home, which it calls its semi-independent living program. A resident manager spends the night in the house, which holds six females, ages 16 to 18. The house is often empty during the day as residents attend local public schools or hold part-time jobs.

The per diem cost for the home is a third of the RTC cost. Laura could share a room with another older teen and would be responsible for preparing her own meals, doing her own laundry, shopping, and housekeeping. The house supervisor conducts life skills classes several times during the week and can spend one-on-one time with Laura as she works through several self-sufficiency workbooks. The staff will help Laura find her own place to live shortly before she is 18 and discharged from the system.

Example #2

Stan lives in a group home with 14 other males, ages 13 to 18. He is close to 17 and is really tired of the antics of his younger housemates. He has a hard time getting up for work when the younger kids stay awake until 3 A.M. nightly playing video games. The agency operating the group home opens a smaller "transition home," which is basically a home in town with four bedrooms and a finished basement.

Stan is one of the first clients to move to the house and shares a room with another youth whose family is nonexistent. Two social workers take turns sleeping at the house and soon the house is full with four pairs of roommates. The youth know that they have a lot of freedom, but will be moved back into the group home if they break too many rules. Weekly group meetings help resolve roommate conflicts and allow residents to confront each other about complaints or clashes in life styles. Stan can stay at the house until he is 18 and needs to start saving money for a deposit on his own place.

Example #3

Le'Andre is 17-years-old and delinquent with a history of stealing cars. He is referred to a transitional living group home (TLGH) as an alternative to a correctional facility. He is involved in a power struggle with his parents. Dad is schizophrenic and mom is extremely rigid. The constant instability of the family makes it necessary for him to be placed out of his home.

Le'Andre is interviewed and accepted. While in the TLGH, he works, goes to school, and cooperates with house rules. He transitions successfully to an individual apartment in the same agency's scattered-site apartment program.

Thirteen years later, he buys a new, $95,000 house in an inner city neighborhood. He is a welder and is married with one child. He was a perfect candidate for a group home, willing to cooperate and accept reasonable structure that did not exist in his own home. Many youth his age are "beyond" structured settings, having seen too many group settings, and are weary of the idea of living with more strangers.

Advantages

- Youth in an affiliated RTC can move into a home and still have contact with former staff/counselors.

- RTCs can build self-sufficiency preparation into their weekly activities.

- RTCs often are associated with well-established agencies with many connections, large endowments, and a fundraising system in place that could be harnessed to obtain furnishings, supplies, and cash for start-up.

- Group homes provide more supervision and social contacts and may be more "normal" than living alone at 17.

- Can be a safe place to live.

- Can be less expensive than individual apartments, if kept full.

- Can provide more of an open community experience than an RTC.

- Has a much smaller population than an RTC.

Disadvantages

- Group and crowd control issues can be a problem.

- Need for 24-hour supervision.

- One bad apple ...

- Is probably not in neighborhood where youth will live at discharge.
- Youth get used to having staff guide their behavior.
- Not a long-term postdischarge living arrangement possibility.
- Limited in size.
- Might require double-coverage/high-fixed costs.

Other Observations

- The key to a good transitional home is the quality of the staff and the mix of youth.
- It's important to be flexible enough to provide for different treatment needs in the same facility.
- Location is important.
- A placement is not a "fit" without a youth's cooperation.

9
Shelters

"Chris, it sounds like you really can't go home again. This is the third time you've been here this month. Your mom's crack addiction isn't going to end soon. I'm going to call the county and see if we can find a safer place for you. With your job and school success, I think you probably could make it on your own with a little help."

A shelter is a facility that provides short-term emergency housing to teens in crisis

Examples

Example #1

Walter is a 16-year-old who shows up at the runaway shelter due to his alcoholic father's abusiveness. He makes it clear that he can't go home again. He fears his father will hurt him seriously the next time. After an investigation, the local child services investigators agree with Walter. He is placed in custody and remains at the shelter until a long-term placement is found. The county cannot find a foster home willing to take in a teenage boy.

After three weeks, the county finds a program willing to give Walter a try in their new supervised semi-independent living program located in a five-unit apartment building about 20 minutes from the shelter. The county caseworker assures the ILP that the shelter has agreed to take Walter back, temporarily, if the placement doesn't work out.

Example #2

Dianne lives in her own apartment supervised by a private ILP. After several months of progress, Dianne starts to slip and begins missing school and other appointments. Dianne's history of depression concerns the ILP staff and they feel something needs to be done. Dianne's last depression led to a suicide attempt.

Dianne is taken to the local psychiatric hospital, where, after a three-hour evaluation, she is released back to the ILP staff. The hospital feels she does not need to be hospitalized at this point. ILP staff take Dianne to the agency's youth crisis center, where she can be supervised 24 hours a day. A referral is made the next day to a therapist she had seen in the past and Dianne agrees to stay at the shelter for the next 10 days. The daily contact with staff and the meetings with her therapist help a lot. Dianne and ILP staff meet at the shelter and work out an agreement where she would return to her apartment, call the ILP every morning when she arrived at school, come to the ILP office after school, and meet her therapist.

Since Dianne was going to be discharged from the system in four months, everyone agreed that a return to a long-term supervised placement would not help her develop the coping skills needed to adjust to life on her own. ILP staff met to discuss other ways to get Dianne connected to people and resources that could help her once out of the program.

Example #3

Quincy was ready to leave the group home he lived in for the last 12 months. Although he was almost 18, his caseworker knew he was not ready for the freedom and responsibility of his own apartment, but he needed real-life experience to help him realize what he didn't know. Quincy immediately caused problems by playing loud music at night and having friends over at all hours. After several warnings, he was picked up at his apartment and taken to the local youth shelter. He couldn't believe ILP staff would make him stay at the shelter with all of the "young brats," and he threatened to run away. ILP staff assured him that if he ran from the shelter he would be terminated from the program and not have a chance to get his own apartment back. After five days in the shelter, he began begging the ILP for another chance. ILP staff wrote up a three-week contract, with Quincy's input, that stated the terms for him to follow in order to keep his apartment.

Two days after his return to his apartment, the landlord called to complain about damages Quincy and his friends had done to the apartment during a rowdy party. ILP staff went over and picked Quincy up, took him back to the shelter, where he remained until his eighteenth birthday. Since he showed little sign of cooperating with the ILP, he was terminated from care and he and his possessions were taken to the house of one of his partying friends.

Advantages

- Might be a community's only option.
- Helpful in transitions to and from less restrictive settings.
- Can have staff who connect youth with needed resources.
- A great backup for a scattered-site program.
- Some shelters allow for long-term residence.
- Can be flexible in deciding quickly who can stay.
- Can have staff experienced in connecting quickly with troubled youth.

Disadvantages

- Usually have time-limited stays.
- Often can be crowded.
- Might not be as helpful if the shelter is run by a different agency than yours.
- Can put youth in contact with high-risk or predatory youth.

- Youth can come in contact with other transient and troubled youth.
- Smaller communities usually do not have shelters.

Other Observations

- Shelter staff often act as service brokers for youth in trouble.

10
Subsidized Housing

 "Stan, tell your friends not to wash their cars in your parking lot. The water here at Death Valley Apartments is expensive."

Subsidy programs provide youth with a monthly stipend that can be used towards a self-chosen living arrangement, food, and personal supplies, while the youth follows certain agency guidelines.

Note: All independent living arrangements are in some way "subsidized." The examples discussed in this chapter are situations in which the housing units are operated by large rental management companies receiving some source of government funding.

Examples

Example #1

Talesha was doing poorly in the ILP. She refused to go to school or meet with her tutor. She didn't want to work and put little effort in keeping her place clean. She tried to get others to do things for her and didn't seem to care at all that she has only two months' time in the system left. Talesha didn't believe that the welfare system had changed and stated that she would find some way for "the system" to support her.

ILP staff went ahead and put her on a subsidized housing waiting list. When her two months were up, Talesha didn't have anyplace to go. An apartment became available at the last minute. ILP staff took some money out of Talesha's program savings account and prepaid three months of rent to her new landlord, the housing agency. She was assisted in finding used furniture and basic supplies and moved out of her apartment into the subsidized apartment. She couldn't believe how much nicer her ILP apartment was. Staff explained again that if she failed to hold a job and to convince the landlord of her apartment that she was responsible, she would lose her new place and have to fend for herself.

Example #2

Sharon was a teen mom who recently was released from a correctional institution. The plan was for her to move into her own apartment for three months to prove that she was now more responsible and then her child would join her. Sharon did surprisingly well in her own apartment, holding a job and attending GED classes at the same time. Her child moved in with her after three months. She proved to be a competent mother, but was running out of time in custody. ILP staff placed her on a subsidized housing waiting list on her eighteenth birthday. She would be allowed to stay in care until an apartment became available. Meanwhile, child care issues would need to be worked out.

A month later, a unit was available. ILP staff helped her move her furniture into her new place and paid her deposit. From her previous job she had saved enough money to cover two months' rent. She would need to find a way to get her child to day care to keep her job.

Advantages

- Might be your only choice.
- Can be affordable even for part-time employees.
- Locations can be in many parts of the city.
- Might be good possibility for teen moms who can't work full-time.

- Can be a long-term housing situation for youth whose issues make it hard for them to obtain and sustain a full-time job.

Disadvantages

- Can lack a choice of location.
- Property is not always in the best part of town.
- Can be located in dilapidated public housing complexes.
- Maintenance might be slow in coming.
- Waiting lists can be long.
- Might not exist outside of larger cities.
- Client might have to be 18 before an application can even be started.
- Management might lack "pride of ownership."
- No structure or daily supervision.

Other Observations

- Can give the youth a distorted impression of the true cost of housing.
- Luck of the draw can determine quality of the apartment.

"Lance, you know your uncle Freddie can't stay here. You signed a lease that states only one person lives here. The neighbors and the landlord have complained to us about his daily presence here and his drinking problem. It doesn't help that he sings cowboy songs when he's drunk, either. We can help you find a place for him to stay, but if you don't cooperate, then you'll have to move out."

11
Residential Treatment Centers

"OK, which one of you took my shaving cream! I work. I make money. You all spend your life trying to be the next Bart Simpson. I'm too old to be around all of you 14-year-old zeros. Three more months and I'm outa here. And don't come runnin' to my crib when you get put on house arrest! You'll never get to level four!"

A residential treatment center (RTC) is a facility or group of facilities that usually serve between 15 to 40 youth and that utilize a combination of on-grounds and community-based services, with many services provided on-site.

Examples

Example #1

George had been in custody in the Hilltop RTC since he was 15 1/2 and was responding positively to the center's program. He was now seven months from his eighteenth birthday, when due to budget restrictions, he would be discharged from care and on his own. The Hilltop staff knew that George could not return home, as his father was still incarcerated and his mom, addicted to crack. One of the youth workers was assigned to help George complete a workbook on self-sufficiency and a life skills training program. George was resistant initially, but eventually liked the meetings and the one-on-one time with the youth worker.

As his birthday approached, Hilltop staff started asking around for donations of furniture and furnishings and were able to gather enough stuff to fully furnish an apartment. They also helped George find a job in the community and he saved enough for a deposit. George and the youth worker eventually found a landlord willing to give him a try in his own apartment on the good faith that George would keep his job. After his eighteenth birthday, staff held a moving party and moved George into his new place. Even though George was officially out of Hilltop and the child welfare system, the staff keep regular contact with him and invite him over for meals from time to time.

Example #2

Kyle has made outstanding progress in the Riverside Residential Treatment Center. His caseworker knows he needs to move to a less structured setting to begin learning how to function more independently. Kyle's cognitive limitations (IQ of 67) raise concerns about his ability to live alone. Riverside staff recommend their new transitional group home. Kyle moved into the home, which is owned by Riverside, but is located five miles away. Kyle and five other young men share space in the house and attend weekly life skills groups and cooking classes. On Saturdays, the live-in resident manager oversees chores and leads a one-hour house meeting. Kyle takes a bus to school and has a 12-hour-a-week job. His ILP social worker visits him weekly, as does his tutor. When Kyle is 18, he will be assisted in finding affordable housing and probably will be connected in some way to the adult Mental Retardation and Developmental Disability system.

Advantages

- RTCs are often part of well-established organizations with many available resources on site.

- RTCs can act as the back-up plan for a youth who left the RTC to go to a less restrictive setting and had too many problems.

- RTCs can build life skills training into their daily services.

- Trained RTC staff can address separation and loss issues with youth who live on grounds, before they move to a less restrictive setting.

- RTCs can develop their own continuum of care to which a youth can move after leaving the RTC. RTC staff can make a model such as a scattered-site apartment program part of their aftercare process.

- Can have top notch facilities.

- Youth come in contact with a variety of professionals and caring adults.

Disadvantages

- RTCs are often two to four times as expensive as less restrictive models.

- There are many people who staff an RTC, all of whom can be involved with a youth. After leaving an RTC, a youth who has connected with these people will have to make a quick or instant adjustment to life without any of them.

- Youth who adjust to an RTC might not be able to adjust to a less supervised setting in the time available.

- Youth in RTCs must follow rules that exist for the benefit of the group and might be based on rules that don't exist in real life.

- RTC staff might focus too much on the present and past and not enough on the future.

- Some RTCs are wonderful places with all kinds of amenities, such as a cafeteria, a gym, a swimming pool and laundry services—all of which disappear the day a youth moves out.

- RTC staff who best know a youth might discontinue contact as soon as the youth leaves the RTC.

- The RTC might not be in a neighborhood where a youth can live after discharge from care

- A focus on group control can dominate treatment.

Other Observations

- Will some RTCs disappear due to managed care initiatives?

Part II, Housing Issues, looks at the challenges ILP staff face in their decisionmaking. Some of these challenges are practical, such as making arrangements for moving; others are more complicated, such as funding concerns.

Part II: Housing Issues

12
Operational Issues

"Cecilia, your lease specifically says no pets allowed. I'm going to take your iguana home with me until you find someone else to keep it. I hope it fits in my van!"

Developing and operating any one of the models discussed in Part I takes time, patience, and openness on the part of everyone in a local child welfare/juvenile justice system. There are, however, practical issues that cut across all models, which we will address in this chapter. It really helps to learn from the experience of other programs before you start developing new housing options. Even though the ILP field is relatively new, there are dozens of programs around the country that have been up and running for some time now. (A list of possible resource people is in Appendix A.)

Intake

Nobody knows how a youth will respond to being placed in any particular living arrangement. Teens always have their own agendas and will try to steer events in a way that benefits them. Some youth send a clear message that they do not want to become self-sufficient and would prefer that someone provide for them. As discussed earlier, most youth either remain at home, return home after unsuccessfully trying to make it on their own, or are heavily subsidized by parents for years after they move out. Youth in the system don't have this luxury. They will be placed in the position of providing for themselves even if they resist this reality every step of the way.

Below are some of the issues that you should consider when deciding the most appropriate living arrangement for a youth referred to an ILP.

- Many, if not all, youth referred to ILPs are far from being ready to take full responsibility for their lives. If young adults from normal families are not totally independent until their mid-20s, the same should be expected of youth in the child welfare system. Youth are placed in less restrictive settings such as individual scattered-site apartments, not because they are ready, but because budget limitations will force them to face life on their own soon after their eighteenth birthday (in most states) whether they are ready or not.

- Many youth with numerous risk factors do well in ILPs. Many youth with few risk factors do poorly. The reasons for success and failure in any model are numerous and complex. Some bright youth deliberately sabotage their progress to buy more time in the system. Some capable youth get into drugs; some limited youth seem loaded with common sense and an ability to bond with numerous supportive adults.

- "Failures," such as becoming pregnant, losing a job, getting evicted, or being arrested for criminal activities can serve as a wake-up call to youth in ILPs and can be used by staff to teach important lessons and turn a youth's life around.

- Look at the recentness, frequency, and severity of criminal activities when evaluating a youth for your ILP. Some youth build up lengthy court records in their early teens and then stop negative actions when removed from a dysfunctional family. Some youth who commit onetime severe crimes, such as felonious assault or grand theft, stop these activities upon entering treatment for chemical dependency.

- The same applies for mental health issues. Some youth with a past history of suicide attempts or hospitalization for unusual behavior change significantly with medication or therapy and never show symptoms again. If an episode of depression or suicidal ideation is fairly recent, then care should be given to gather an updated assessment by a psychologist or psychiatrist who will sign a letter stating that a youth is ready or not ready for a particular IL living arrangement.

- Pregnant or parenting teens can do well in any living arrangement. The event of becoming pregnant or having a baby can serve to focus a previously "wild" youth on family survival and future planning issues. But these clients need to understand that they have to continuously prove that they are able to handle the responsibility of parenting to remain in less restrictive settings.

- School progress does not always correlate with IL success. Some youth in ILPs will chose to drop out of school to earn enough money to support themselves when cut off from care. This might indeed be the best thing to do, even though it lowers a program's educational success rate.

- Age is not necessarily an intake issue at all. Some 16-year-olds referred to ILPs for restrictive settings are often mature beyond their years and know when to ask for help. Some 18-year-olds might never be able to function without outside support.

Necessary Rules and Policies

The more clear and up front the expectations of a program are to a youth and his/her care providers, the better the chance that things will go smoothly. Having written rules and policies in place is absolutely necessary to prevent clients from the old "nobody ever said I couldn't have a toga party" situation. Most programs start out with a list of common sense rules for clients to follow, and then add on more detailed rules as clients come up with more creative ways to keep staff busy. Listed below are topics that most programs address in client policy manuals.

- Education requirements
- Apartment cleanliness expectations

- Work expectations
- Communication responsibilities
- Responsibilities as a tenant
- Savings requirements
- Use/control of utilities
- Personal safety guidelines
- Use of phone
- Visitor limitations
- Budgeting expectations
- Emergency procedures
- Care of furnishings
- Medical problems
- Procedures for decorating apartments/rooms
- Disciplinary measures and consequences
- Use and/or ownership of cars
- Child care/babysitting guidelines
- Illegal activities
- Grounds for early termination
- Lending/borrowing money
- Keeping appointments
- Unauthorized purchases
- Pregnancy notification
- Harboring runaways/friends/family members
- Curfew expectations
- Rights to furnishings/supplies upon discharge

- Communication with staff expectations

It might be helpful to have a new client read the program policies out loud, to eliminate the excuse of ignorance. The policies should make it clear what is expected, as well as what the consequences will be for breaking a policy. Also, make sure a new client signs a form which states that s/he has read and understands the policies and agrees to follow them.

Most programs look for ways to keep youth in the program, not for reasons to get rid of them. A general rule is that most youth will break some of the rules, some of the time. If a youth breaks all of the rules some of the time, or one of the rules all of the time, then consequences should follow, such as placement in a more restrictive setting or discharge from the program.

Using the Continuum

As discussed, no one can predict how a youth will handle his or her first venture in independent living. Some youth will be in over their heads immediately and will need to be moved, maybe temporarily, into a more supervised settings. Ideally, a youth will move in the direction of more restrictive to less restrictive settings. A lot depends on what options an agency has in place. Remember that it can take years to create a full continuum of living arrangements. Here are some examples of how a continuum could be utilized.

Example #1

At 17, Bill was discharged from a residential treatment center. Since he was going to be cut off from state support on his eighteenth birthday, his caseworker wanted him to gain some experience in living independently.

Bill was referred to an ILP who helped him locate a one-bedroom apartment near where he would attend school. Bill started off well, but soon began to have problems when school friends got word that he had his own place. The landlord and ILP staff met with Bill to discuss the situation and gave him a warning that further problems could lead to his eviction. After a raucous Saturday night party resulted in several calls to the landlord from other tenants, the landlord called the ILP and asked that Bill be removed. The ILP was part of an agency that also ran a shelter for youth. A surprised Bill and his possessions were taken to the shelter and Bill was told to continue going to school and to follow the rules of the shelter.

The ILP made a three-week contract with Bill, stating that if he followed the shelter rules and terms of the contract, he would be given another chance in his own apartment. Bill disliked living with a large group of younger teens and couldn't wait to get out of the shelter. He met the terms of the contract, was moved into another apartment near his school, and made sure not to tell his school friends where he lived. The ILP moved a quieter youth into the original apartment, as the landlord knew that the program was not the cause of the troubles.

Example #2

Jenny was living in a group home and everyone felt she had really matured a lot from the experience. Her caseworker knew that Jenny would be on her own when cut off from state support at 18. Jenny was afraid to live on her own, and a local ILP offered to find a host home for her. She moved in with the host, a former foster mother, and really liked the experience. After six months with the host she felt she was ready to try to live in her own place, which she knew she would eventually have to do anyway.

Jenny spent the last five months in her own apartment, while still maintaining contact with her host on weekends. When Jenny was discharged from the system, she was able to keep her apartment, the security deposit, and all of the supplies and furnishings given to her by the agency. Her new job and savings from previous jobs would help her meet her rent and utility bills.

Example #3

Teara was released from a state correctional facility and had no place to call home. She was placed in a semi-independent group home with four other girls run by a nonprofit organization. She met with her parole officer weekly and attended weekly support groups. She also met weekly with her ILP social worker to discuss her progress and work on life skills projects. After three months in the group home, Teara was given a chance to live in her own apartment. She did well on her own but as discharge was approaching, it became obvious that she would not be able to cover the rent for her current apartment.

As soon as she turned 18, she went to apply for a subsidized apartment through a local low-cost housing agency. She was placed on a waiting list and continued to work and attend GED classes. The state correctional system agreed to support her until a low-cost apartment became available. When an opening came for a subsidized apartment, the ILP staff helped her move again. Two years later, Teara called the ILP and said she was still at the same location.

Example #4

Felix was in a foster home for the past two years. As he approached 16, everyone involved felt that he needed to become more self-sufficient, as he could not return to live with his family. He was referred to an ILP that placed him in his own apartment. He had endless problems and couldn't seem to handle the freedom or responsibility of being on his own. His caseworker felt that returning him to his foster home would send the wrong message. Instead he was placed in a shared home, a small house owned by the ILP's parent agency that had three beds and a live-in resident manager employed by the ILP. Felix didn't like his roommates and expressed continuously his desire to get out of the shared home. He agreed to follow a three-week contract that he helped design to get another chance on his own.

He blew his contract during the second week by not coming home. He couldn't believe that the ILP held him to the contract and wouldn't let him move out. He was placed on another three-week contract. This time around he followed it and was assisted in finding another apartment. He was obligated to cover the deposit on the second apartment and was told that if he was evicted from this apartment he would lose his own investment. Since he was near 18, he also was told that if evicted from this apartment, he would have to inform his caseworker and ILP staff where to deliver his belongings.

Example #5

Angela was referred to the ILP by her county caseworker, who felt she needed to learn to live on her own. Angela was placed in her own apartment but was soon asked to leave due to too many visitors and late night noise. The ILP had a contract with a local boarding home for women near the city center. Angela resisted the move and said she would run away if placed there. ILP staff and her caseworker pointed out that it was her choice to run or give the boarding home a try. She agreed to give it a week. She was given her own room but needed to share bathroom and shower facilities with others on her floor.

Angela caught the bus to her GED program each day and found a job downtown. After two weeks, she told ILP staff that the place wasn't all that bad and she liked living downtown. Angela met another young woman at the boarding home and asked the ILP if she could move out with her new friend. ILP staff agreed that if she continued to follow rules, work, and attend GED classes, they would consider this plan. Angela was also told that she would have to save for the deposit with her friend. They both worked extra hours and soon saved enough for a deposit. Angela's ILP social worker helped her find a landlord willing to rent to two young woman, with the ILP as co-signer. Angela's friend agreed to sign a contract with the ILP, stating that she would follow the program rules.

When Angela turned 18, she was given two months to find full-time work and save some money. After two months, ILP staff met with Angela, her friend, and the landlord, and it was decided that the landlord would allow the two young women to continue living in his apartment, even though the ILP's name was taken off the lease. To assure that the deal go through, ILP made Angela and her friend agree to prepay the rent for two months to show their commitment to the landlord.

Example #6

Edward at 17 has been involved in the social services system for 12 years. He is from a family where the father was alcoholic and extremely physically abusive. Ed had been in placement since he was 12 and is hyperactive and aggressive. He averages about two placements per year and at 17 is referred to an ILP. The program accepts him and initially places him in a rooming house.

Although Ed is charming and social, he engages in power struggles with the rooming house manager and is asked to leave within two weeks. The other two rooming houses used by the ILP are Ed's next two placements, with Ed living in one for three months and the other for one month before being asked to leave. At this point, Ed is told he has to find his own living arrangement and the ILP will decide whether he can live there. Ed lives in a variety of roommate situations, host homes, shared apartments. He has 13 living arrangements over 24 months. He stays out of the criminal justice system, however, and at 19 is on his own. Throughout the two-year period, the only constant in Ed's life is the ILP.

There are youth who are going to have a tough time living anywhere due to their behavior, but an ILP can be flexible enough to support them even through turbulent times. There are some youth who don't "fit" anywhere but still need support and guidance. A good ILP can provide that.

Establishing Back-Up Plans

Again, no one knows how a particular youth will respond to placement in any specific living arrangement. Youth with potential can get caught up in issues that make it impossible for them to live alone. Youth with limitations can be highly responsible and have fewer problems than youth in honors programs. Thus, there has to be a plan in place to relocate a youth who is having chronic problems at their living arrangement.

ILPs must know at the initial interview where a youth will go if a placement doesn't work out. Keeping an unruly youth in a privately owned apartment increases the risk of damages and bad public relations. Many programs keep the lease in their name to be able to remove a tenant on short notice.

Public Relations

Needless to say, youth and young adults living away from 24-hour adult supervision will create situations that need staff intervention. Loud music, parties, drug use, relatives who move in, hygienically deficient clients, gang involvement, etc., are part of the daily work of anyone working in the field. Talk with a college resident manager or a landlord in a university neighborhood and you'll find little difference between the antics of IL clients and young adults from "normal" families.

Many landlords prefer renting to someone associated with a program that keeps an eye on them, rather than to a couple of college freshman 300 miles from ma and pa for the first time.

There are some things to keep in mind when dealing with situations where things have gotten out of hand:

- The landlord is always right. Unless a landlord is blatantly guilty of discrimination, sexual harassment, or criminal involvement, it's best to keep him/her happy. Even one negative letter to the editor or news item can damage a program for some time. Keeping a landlord happy might mean removing a problem client immediately, leaving your quiet house in the middle of a night to break up a party, or starting out Monday morning on your hands and knees cleaning up a trashed apartment.

  Most agencies using scattered-site apartments have been able to find landlords willing to give a youth a try, if they are assured they will not be left with a mess or lengthy and expensive eviction proceedings. But landlords don't want to be taken advantage of or asked to be "understanding " of this poor teen who has a past history of abuse and neglect. Landlords want three things: rent on time, no problems, and if there are problems, an immediate response.

- Most child welfare agencies experience some type of negative publicity over the years. The larger the agency, the higher the odds of bad things happening. However, an ILP that places youth in solo living arrangements can be accused of being too harsh or outright foolish. Sometimes it's necessary to explain that this arrangement was made out of necessity, due to the fact that this youth is getting cut off from support at 18.

- Sending a consistent message to all other care providers, landlords, neighbors etc., is important. Here's a sample:

  > We never are 100% sure how a youth will do when out on his/her own for the first time. I wish we had more time to help these youth adjust to life on their own, but we don't. Our clients are going to make all of the mistakes that young adults make, plus a few others. We do our best to help them, but problems will arise. We're trying to make the best of a bad situation. Call us as soon as you see even a potential problem and we'll look into it. If it's obvious that this situation won't work, we'll try another living arrangement option. Thanks for your patience.

- The real key to public relations is to prepare all involved for the best and worst that could happen and enlist their help in making things right. Don't allow other system professionals to sit back and watch the chaos. Ask for their ideas, observations, and support.

- If you do build up a positive track record, make sure that everyone knows about it. After a while, people will know that your program is good but can only do so much. Celebrate your successes, but share your humanness when things go wrong; remember—the person criticizing your efforts just might have a 13-year-old at home ready to express his/her independence in new and annoying ways.

- In group living situations, such as a supervised apartment program, it is wise to contact neighbors regularly to see if they have any complaints. Problems should be addressed immediately. Christmas cards or flowers can help too!

- Selling the idea of placing a youth alone is a neverending PR project. Every new person entering the system will probably need to learn about the program's long-term goals and previous successes.

Roommates

Some programs assume youth will share rooms or apartments to cover program expenses. Some agencies refuse roommate situations intentionally, not just to avoid the inevitable squabbling, but also to give a youth a real chance to mange his/her own space, time, money, etc., without being able to blame problems on someone else. Some youth simply can't compromise or adjust to another person's style or needs. Spending all of your time mediating roommate disputes might be less important than helping a youth feel the weight of individual responsibility.

In bigger cities, rents are often so high that programs need per diems coming in for two clients in order to make the numbers work. Here are some examples of different possible roommate scenarios.

Example #1

Chuck has been living for a year in his own apartment since shortly after his sixteenth birthday. He has been a responsible tenant and never seems to miss a day of school or work. His best friend Larry's parents are moving out of town and Larry really wants to graduate from the high school he and Chuck attend. Chuck approached ILP staff about the possibility of Larry moving in with Chuck. ILP staff discuss this with the referring county social worker who agrees that Chuck has been nothing but competent in his stay in the ILP.

The ILP social worker asks the landlord if this would be possible, and he feels that Chuck taking on a roommate would be worth a try. Larry signs a contract stating that he will pay half of the security deposit, follow the ILP rules as well as the landlord's, and pay half of the rent and utility bill. Larry also signs an agreement that he could be removed from this situation if problems arose. Four months later, it's obvious that this was a good decision. Chuck will leave the system with a fully furnished apartment with half of his bills covered by his roommate and best friend. The county and ILP agree that maybe this situation could occur again.

Example #2

Tamika moved into her own apartment at 17 and did really well in the program. As the end of her time in the system approached, she asked ILP staff if she could have a roommate. She had grown close to another young woman in her complex who had a full-time job and was extremely responsible. ILP staff ran the idea by the referring county agency caseworker who thought it was worth a try. After several conversations, a written agreement was signed by the nonprogram roommate who agreed to cover half of the security deposit, pay half of the rent, and follow the ILP rules. The roommate understood that she could be asked to leave if things didn't work out. A year later, the two were still doing well together with occasional squabbles over boyfriends.

Example #3

Pamela was three months away from termination and was pregnant by Pete. Pam had a good paying part-time job and Pete was nearing his second year at the factory. Pam asked if Pete could move in with her. The ILP social worker met with the two and was impressed with their planning, communication, and persistence. It was clear that they had a potential long-term relationship and Pete was dead set on being a good father. The ILP couldn't let Pete move in while Pam was in custody but met with the landlord who agreed to give the couple a try. Pete moved in with Pam a day after she was discharged from care, having co-signed the new lease with Pam.

Dealing with Landlords

Most programs utilizing the scattered- or cluster-site models have been able to find landlords willing to give the youth and the program a try.

Obviously, it might take some salesmanship to convince a landlord to rent to a 16-year-old with a pieced eyebrow and an attitude. But most landlords deal with the "general public" and have endless stories about adult tenants from hell.

It's helpful to give a prospective landlord a written description of the program, a copy of the client policy manual, a 24-hour phone number, and a letter stating the program's possible need to get out of lease.

Here's a sample letter:

Dear Landlord,

The Independent Living Program of Millennium Youth Services is a program designed to provide adolescents who are unable to live at home with a safe place to live, support, and training from a professional staff.

The program has been in existence since 1980 and has served more than 400 youth. The youth in our program have rules to follow, constructive activities to attend, and people to hold them accountable. Our clients are trained in basic independent living skills and job readiness from the moment they enter the program until they are discharged.

Our staff meets with the clients at least twice a week and monitors the client's health, apartment cleanliness, financial situation, and school/work progress. Clients receive a weekly allowance from the program to cover food and transportation.

The Agency will sign the lease*, pay the deposit and monthly rent, cover utilities, and provide a phone and furnishings. If necessary, the program staff will confront any negative behavior in the apartment through verbal confrontation, an allowance deduction, or termination from the program.

---

* Some programs find landlords who allow the youth to sign the lease or have month-to-month rental agreements.

Note: Public agencies usually can't enter into private lease agreements and thus either find landlords willing to allow a youth to sign the lease alone or find a private agency to handle the placement and sign the lease.

In the event an apartment should become vacated prior to the expiration of the lease, Millennium reserves the right to place another client in the apartment, with your approval, of course. If a client terminates early and the ILP has no one to move into the apartment, we would like to be able to get out of the lease by forfeiting the deposit and covering any damages.

If a client successfully completes our program and is ready to take financial responsibility, we release the deposit to them and allow them to keep the apartment, after, of course, clearing this with the landlord.

If there are any questions please call 634-5789.

Risk Management

The entire field of child welfare is a risky business. Kids run away from secure facilities. Youth deal drugs out of residential treatment centers with 24-hour supervision. Girls get pregnant while living in group homes with 24-hour supervision. Allegations of abuse are made against the best foster parents. Fights break out in detention centers with well-trained staff on duty.

There's no way around it: when you deal with at-risk youth, you are at risk yourself. In the field of ILP, you must deal with the reality that many youth in IL programs are not developmentally ready or mature enough to handle the freedom and responsibility of living on their own. But that's what is going to happen and it's up to ILP staff to do what they can with a youth in the given amount of time.

Keys to Risk Management and Avoiding Trouble in General

- **Effective screening:** Don't accept youth with no chance of succeeding in your available living arrangements unless all understand this is a last-chance situation.

- **Documentation:** Keep a written record of visits, phone contacts, meetings, incidents, observations, potential problems, and action taken.

- **Clear policies and procedures:** Have youth sign to verify that he/she understands and agrees to follow your written rules and policies.

- **Signed agreements:** Keep a document that verifies that this living arrangement is court supported.

- **Clear emergency procedures:** Have an on-call and emergency system in place and make sure the youth knows how to access it.

- **Liability insurance:** To cover property damage or personal injury.

- **Back-up plans:** Know where a youth can go immediately, if necessary. Create and use a continuum of living arrangement options that fits your community.

- **Quick confrontation of problems:** If you think something is wrong, it probably is.

- **Frequent contact with referring agency caseworker to discuss daily activities of problem client:** Make sure that everyone involved with the youth knows when problems occur. Don't try to create unrealistic expectations about what your program can do.

- **Mandatory counseling:** AA meetings, prenatal clinics, etc., for youth with special needs.

- **Contracts:** When a youth falters, create a written contract that spells out what is necessary for him or her to remain in the current living arrangement.

- **Daily contact with high-risk clients:** Have a depressed client come to your office after school or have a staff person make daily visits to a client with a medical problem.

- **Regular checks on youth at their living arrangement:** A mix of set and random visits is recommended.

- **Make sure you have complete referral information** to anticipate client problems or areas of concern.

Why Landlords Like Us

- We guarantee rent.

- We have tighter rules than their own.

- We are on-call 24/7/365 for crises.

- We cover damages.

- We handle confrontations.

- We clean up messes.

- We evict, if necessary, without court involvement.

- We limit visitors.

- We have a steady flow of "renters."

- We monitor and supervise our clients.

- **Use electronic monitoring** devices for high-risk clients

- **Hire "life coaches"** to meet daily with lower functioning youth.

- **Assign "trackers"** to check on daily activities of delinquent youth.

- **Find mentors, volunteers, and student interns** to back up ILP staff supervision of clients.

Risk Factors to Consider in Screening Clients

- The client has committed a felony offense in last year.

- The client is chemically dependent.

- The client is pregnant.

- The client has a child.

- The client has more than one child.

- The client has made a suicide attempt in the last year.

- The client has history of poor judgment.

- The client has chronic medical issues.

- The client has chronic mental health issues.

- The client is on psychotropic medication.

- The client has committed more than two misdemeanors in last year.

- The client has run away from a stable placement in the last year.

- The client has little or no work experience in the private sector.

- The client has been violent toward people in last year.

- The client has committed a sex offense in last two years.

- The client has a chronic history of truancy or school problems.

- The client has no known social supports.

- The client has limited intellectual abilities.

- The client avoids responsibilities.

- The client cannot read or write.

- The client has a diagnosed developmental disability.

- The client has friends/family members involved in illegal activities.

Common Problems

You know you're heading for trouble when:

- your client misses two appointments in a row.

- you receive a second complaint from a landlord.

- your client suddenly has new clothing, jewelry, stereo equipment, and no job.

- your client loses a lot of weight in a short period of time.

- your client doesn't come in to get allowance or subsidy money.

- your client goes out of his way to impress you more than once.

- someone other than your client answers the phone and says your client doesn't live there anymore.

- a landlord complains of a steady stream of adult visitors coming to your client's apartment.

- your client gets involved after hours with someone from the child welfare system.

- your client can't sleep for more than three nights in a row.

- your client never leaves his/her apartment.

- your client has less furniture every time you visit.

- your client's landlord shows up at your house.

- the tenants in your client's building show up at your office.

- your client drives a nicer car than your boss.

- the SWAT team is sitting outside of your client's building when you arrive to check his place.

- your client loses a structured activity, such as school or a job.

- you find yourself avoiding contact with your client.

- you lose sleep worrying about a client.

- you see a "family reunion this Saturday" sign on your client's door.

- a local group home director thanks you for allowing his boys to spend weekends at your client's apartment.

- your client has a gang initiation handbook on his coffee table.

- your client has members of his/her family who use the apartment address for some reason.

- your client has members of his/her family who are homeless and spend a lot of time at the youth's place.

- your client tells you his band "Overkill" will only practice on Friday nights.

- you can't see the floor on your client's apartment.

- you notice that your client's boyfriend has mail coming to her apartment.

"When I started this ILP job, I couldn't sleep for the first few months. I would wake up in the middle of the night thinking about all of the things that could go wrong in this program. Scott's depressed and might kill himself. Joy is going to get attacked in that neighborhood. Max is going to start dealing drugs again. Angry landlords will storm our office.

But after a while, very little of that happened. And talking to other social workers who work with foster families, group homes, and RTCs, bad incidents are part of our business. There are stretches of time where few negative things happen. But I know one thing for sure: things are never as bad as they seem, and things are never as good as they seem."

13
Practical Issues

 "When a landlord calls with a complaint about a damaged window or a hole in the wall, we tell him/her to fix it and send us the bill. We try to pay for the damages quickly."

Moves

You'll need access to a truck, a two-wheeler, a tarp, and several readily available strong people to help lift couches, dressers, kitchen tables, etc. It takes a full day to set up an apartment in any program model. Most ILPs are using donated or secondhand furniture and supplies. Sometimes a youth will have supplies or furnishings, but usually you'll need to start from scratch.

If your program allows youth to take over apartments upon discharge, then you'll need to set up a new apartment for each new referral. At times, a youth might decide to leave town or live with friends. In this case, a new client can inherit his/her furniture and your staff will be spared a move.

Some ILPs don't allow staff to lift heavy objects. Some hire unemployed clients and pay them well for their help. It's smart to have a friend at a thrift store who will call you when good deals arrive.

Make sure to set phone service up in advance so your client has a phone on the first night, the same with utilities.

Some programs charge clients for any second moves. Some pay unemployed clients to clean up messy apartments and take the payment from the messy client's savings.

Apartment Condition

The landlord and ILP staff should check the condition of all of these items before the client moves in (See Table 1 for a sample checklist). Have the landlord or resident manager sign the checklist. If the building is sold, you might have to convince the new owner that those burn holes were in the rug when you first came to see the place.

Telephones

Some programs have blocks on their client's phones to avoid long-distance charges. Some have the youth pay for the bill and live with the consequences of a high phone bill. It is helpful to identify one person at your local phone company to deal with when setting up phone service in a new location. This will save you time in explaining your program. Most companies will want your agency's address to bill for a minor. Youth can be extremely clever in finding ways around phone blocks. They should be expected to pay for any bill over budget. (Youth these days seem to see extras such as "three-way calling," "caller ID" and "call-waiting" as basic essentials.)

> *"Jeff, we've been trying to reach you but they say your phone has been disconnected."*
>
> *"Yeah, I couldn't pay the bill."*
>
> *"Why not?"*
>
> *"It was high from three calls I made to a psychic hot-line."*
>
> *"What did the psychic say?"*
>
> *"She said I was about to have major difficulties communicating with important people in my life."*

Utilities

Utility bills can cause unplanned problems for any ILP. Some programs budget a fixed amount per month for utilities and expect a youth to pay for bills over the set amount. Some agencies put the bills in the youth's name, some in the agency's name. Be sure to ask in advance

TABLE 1. Apartment Condition Checklist

Item	Condition
Windows	
Screens	
Doors	
Locks	
Faucets: bathroom	
Faucets: kitchen	
Floors	
Carpets	
Smoke alarm	
Walls: living room	
Walls: bedroom	
Walls: bathroom	
Walls: kitchen	
Closets	
Light fixtures	
Toilet	
Mirrors	
Switches	
Electrical outlets	
Refrigerator	
Stove	
Air conditioner	
Mailbox	
Furnace	
Ceiling	
Other Items needing repair	

All items above have been checked out and the condition noted by client, new life staff, and landlord. From this point on, the client _____ is responsible for the upkeep of the apartment and any damages.

Landlord _____ Date _____

ILP staff _____ Date _____

Client _____ Date _____

for the average monthly cost for utilities for a location. Landlords with old heating/air conditioning systems sometimes lower rent and ignore disclosing that a monthly heating bill might be $100.

Endless teaching about turning off appliances when gone or keeping the thermostat at 70 degrees is necessary, especially to those youth who have never lived in a setting where they controlled temperature.

> *"Jessica, why are the burners on your stove on?"*
>
> *"It was too cold in here and the heat wasn't coming on."*
>
> *"Maybe if you put on some long pants and a sweat shirt over your tank top you wouldn't need more heat."*
>
> *"But I like dressing like this."*
>
> *"Do you like $80 utility bills?"*
>
> *"I didn't think the stove was a utility."*

Furnishing and Supplies

Table 2 offers a sample list of basic supplies needed for a new client moving into an individual apartment. Some programs find donors for many of these items.

Damages

Most tenants have something deducted from their security deposits when they leave an apartment. With teens, it's a given. No matter what living arrangement model you chose, expect to pay for some needed repairs. Some programs take money weekly out of a client's savings or allowance and return the balance to a youth upon discharge, minus any damage costs. Some programs budget for 13 months' rent annually and plan on losing the deposit to damages, shortened leases, or by turning the apartment over to a successful client.

If there are major life changes in your client's life, the chances for damages and apartment messiness increase and it's wise to increase your visits to the site.

Other Ideas

- Find volunteer handymen to make minor repairs.
- Have the agency maintenance person do repairs.

TABLE 2. Apartment Start-Up Furnishings and
Supplies List

Furniture:
☐ couch
☐ chair
☐ end table
☐ lamp
☐ bed
☐ mattresses
☐ dresser
☐ kitchen table
☐ kitchen chairs
☐ curtains/shades

Bedroom/Bathroom Supplies:
☐ blankets
☐ sheets
☐ pillows
☐ pillow cases
☐ alarm clock
☐ towels/washcloths

Kitchen Supplies:
☐ silverware
☐ plates
☐ glasses
☐ bowls
☐ cups
☐ spatula
☐ skillet
☐ pots/pans
☐ garbage can
☐ trash bags
☐ broom
☐ mop
☐ bucket
☐ dust pan
☐ measuring cup
☐ sponges
☐ light bulbs
☐ scrubbing pads
☐ cookie sheet

Personal Items:
☐ soap
☐ shampoo
☐ toothbrush
☐ toothpaste
☐ deodorant
☐ aspirin
☐ bandages
☐ thermometer
☐ toilet paper

Other Necessities:

- Set aside a small portion of a client's weekly allowance each week. At discharge, the client receives this amount minus any repair costs.

- Budget a few thousand dollars for damages a year and be happily surprised if you don't need it.

14
Funding and Budget Issues

 "Betsy, when I checked your apartment, the TV, stereo, air-conditioner, and lava lamp were all on. We'll cover $40 of your utility bill, but anything over that is on you."

Finding long-term financial support for an independent living program is no easy feat. Most programs start small, use existing funding in new ways (e.g., county foster care funds), look under every rock, and spend considerable time writing grants to support program activities. How an ILP funds its operations at the start might not be similar to its strategies five years later. Some programs are foundation driven, with all funding coming from one source. Some are per diem driven, with all funds coming from purchase of service contracts.

Here are some of the funding strategies and ways of saving/making money used by ILPs around the country over the last decade:

- Use existing funds targeted for foster and residential care to provide per diems for contracting IL services.

- Obtain local foundation help to purchase and develop property for a supervised apartment program.

- Obtain national foundation help for start-up costs.

- Do a major capital fund drive to purchase or renovate property to become a supervised apartment or shared home program.

- Obtain United Way support for program start-up and operations.

- Work with the state Independent Living coordinator to access Title IV-E funds for client needs and staff training.

- Become Medicaid certified and draw Medicaid dollars for mental health services to clients.

- Have clients pay for part of their room and board or cover the deposit.

- Have clients share apartments to reduce program expenses. Give roommates financial incentives to make it work.

- Use community food banks to purchase bulk food and household supplies.

- Pay former foster parents to maintain weekly contact with former foster child living alone to save ILP staff time and travel costs.

- Find volunteers to go to weekend yard sales to find deals on needed furniture and supplies.

- Have clients help with office coverage, office work, client moves, apartment cleanup, etc.

- Solicit a local church group to donate property, furnishings, and volunteer services.

- Obtain state Title IV-E IL Initiative funds for client training, supplies, and school fees.

- Obtain grants through the HUD/Stewart McKinney Homeless Assistance Act.

- Include a program wish list in your agency's newsletter.

- Find local banks to provide scholarships for ILP graduates.

- Tap city development block grants and city housing department funds for building purchase or development.

- Obtain correctional system grants for creating IL services as alternatives to institutionalization.

- Obtain state department of human services discretionary grants for special projects, such as city- or statewide independent living conferences.

- Obtain Title IV-E IL funds for independent living workbooks for clients, foster parents, and other care providers.

- Increase regular children's services budgets through local tax levies.

- Shift funds from existing government services to children's services.

- Reduce placements to high-cost residential treatment centers and use savings to fund IL services.

- Reduce placements to correctional facilities and use funds for IL services.

- Look for money from private sources: corporate grants/donations, local foundations, national foundations, civic clubs, church groups.

- Use unused church or community properties for office or storage space.

- Conduct fund-raising projects to raise money for apartment furnishings.

- Look for ways to reduce expenditures by getting things for free, e.g., having volunteers conduct life skills classes.

- Look for ways to transfer responsibilities to others, e.g., having clients save for the deposit on an apartment.

- Have a church group furnish an apartment or gather donated furniture.

- Use volunteers or student interns to conduct life skills training, monitor clients in apartment, and do other needed tasks.

- Find corporate groups willing to paint an entire apartment building or do landscaping work on exterior.

TABLE 3. Budget Categories of a Typical ILP Housing Program

Staff salaries	Apartment furnishings
Staff travel	Pager rental
Staff benefits	Moving expenses
Staff training	Start-up supplies
Truck insurance	Smoke detectors, fire extinguishers
Gas/maintenance	Liability insurance
Office rent/utilities	Client allowance (for food, transporta-
Client rents/deposits	tion, laundry, and personal items)
Office supplies	Administrative overhead
Client phone	Apartment insurance
Office telephone	Damages and repair
Client utilities	Equipment rental
Answering service	Miscellaneous

- Contact local hotels, college dorms, department stores, etc., for used beds, furniture, lamps, tables, etc.

- Create training materials and market them to other agencies.

- Ask local sports organizations for tickets to events.

- Allow friends of clients to share apartment and pay half of rent to ILP.

- Make clients pay for all damages or second moves.

- Have staff live on grounds for free instead of paying salaries.

- Have clients do maintenance work, cut grass, paint rooms, etc.

- Transfer tasks to other involved people, i.e., have older sibling take client to get state ID, ask aunt to take client shopping for school clothes.

- Call other ILPs around the country. Don't reinvent the wheel!

TABLE 4. Is There a Better Deal?

Sample Independent Living Program monthly expenses (in the Midwest, based on a six-month stay in the program):

Fixed Expenses	Averages of Fixed Expenses
Rent	$300
Deposit (total divided by six months)	$50
Utilities	$35
Telephone	$35
Start-up food	$20
Start-up furnishings	$30
Start-up supplies (averaged over six months)	$20
Miscellaneous	$50
Moving help	$10
Weekly allowance ($60/week)	$240
Total fixed expenses (monthly average)	**$790**

Per diem = $49

$49 x 30.5 days = $1494.50 amount received for services per month

$1494.50 - $790 (fixed expenses) = $704.50

$704.50 divided by 30.5 days = $23 a day left for staff services

(See Table 5 for a list of typical staff services.)

TABLE 5. Typical Staff Services

Calling schools	Problemsolving about a client
School enrollment	Trouble shooting with a client
Telephone setup	Addressing school problems
Apartment visits	Drug screens
Explaining program	Public relations
Apartment setup	Networking with other agencies
Emergencies: hospital runs	Accounting for petty cash
Getting IDs: birth certificates, social	Looking for supplies
security cards, medical cards	Writing out checks
Medical appointments	Accounting
Apartment maintenance	Answering the phones
Counselor contact	Supervising staff
Intake	Trying to understand teens
Orientation	Putting out "fires"
Life skills training	Worrying about clients
Shopping for food	Pregnancy tests
Shopping for supplies	Parenting classes
Shopping for furniture	Buying baby supplies
Copies of keys	Checking smoke detectors
Reports: weekly and monthly	Transferring bills
Maintaining files	Requests for program information
Court contacts	Reports, reports, reports
Caseworker contacts	Pre-independent living preparation
CASA contacts	Field conferences
Landlord contacts	Truck maintenance
Inservice training	Dealing with relatives
Making up life skills books	Setting up files
Training foster parents	Talking to former clients
Weekly groups	Writing grants
Counseling	Looking for funding
Employment search	Shaking your head
Employer contacts	Looking for good materials
Staff meetings	Cleaning storage area
Program planning	Field reading
Office maintenance	Case discussions
Intake interviews	Training: out of office
Close-out class	Apartment cleaning
Clothing shopping	

15
Supervision and Monitoring Issues

"Compared to what! Sure girls get pregnant in our pro-gram, but they do so in foster homes, group homes, residen-tial treatment centers, jails even. Girls in the 16 to 19 age range have the highest rate of pregnancy worldwide. In the rest of the world, they might have three by now. If they really want to get pregnant, there's not a lot to be done. Maybe we can help them prevent a second pregnancy."

Supervision depends on several factors: the living arrangement cho-sen for a youth, the youth's maturity level, the presence and/or avail-ability of other adults, and the presence/absence of other youth. Some youth seem to need little to no supervision and enjoy the contact and monitoring of adults. Some youth need in-apartment video cameras and electronic monitoring bracelets to keep from breaking rules and laws. Most programs utilize a mix of supervisory strategies that fol-low the client's actions.

The Continuum of Supervisory Strategies

- On-grounds with a live-in adult: e.g, host home, mentor apart-ment, supervised apartments, adult roommate situations.

- Intensive monitoring: daily visits to client's place.

- Semi-intensive monitoring: from two to three visits per week plus daily phone contact.

- Typical monitoring: one to two visits a week at client's place of residence with additional phone contact.

- Less than once-a-week visits with phone contact.

Other Options

- Random, unannounced visits.

- Client must come to office daily.

- Clients must call in daily.

- Volunteers/students visit youth weekly.

- Former foster parents are contracted to monitor their former foster youth.

- Electronic monitoring bracelets for youth on parole or probation.

- Resident managers are enlisted (or hired!) to report client behavior to ILP staff.

- In-house video surveillance cameras (just kidding!).

All ILPs must have a 24-hour, on-call system easily accessed by a client, as well as backup plans, in case a youth can't handle a living arrangement.

16
Staff Issues

"You're right boss, we should have seen that coming. This 16-year-old should have been able to overcome the peer pressure of seven friends ready to party at his apartment. The 'no parties allowed' sign we posted on his living room wall must have come down before we got in our car."

It takes a certain breed of social worker to work in an ILP. Someone looking for a predictable daily routine with a clear sense of what needs to be done will probably feel like they're following Alice in a free fall. Most ILPs are basically designing programs around the needs of individual youth and 20 youth equal 20 mini-programs. IL workers needs to be:

- flexible ("Let's try something else, this tree house program ain't workin'—we forgot to factor in the squirrels.")

- creative (Let's buy a mobile home—then if a client gets evicted, we move it a mile down the road.")

- patient ("Son, that's the twelfth time you lost your key this month. We have this body piercer who will dangle it from your chin....")

- a salesperson ("Mr. Landlord, this young man will be the best investment you've ever made. That six-pointed star tattoo indicates he has a unique destiny.")

- a self-starter ("When I first moved out, I had to wait for hours before Jeeves, our family butler, brought over freshly pressed ascots.")

Also, ILP staff:

- must be able to work independently, as they will be out of office more than in.

- must see themselves in a teaching rather than parental or clinical role, or else a new dependency can be created.

- must have a thorough knowledge of community resources for adolescents and adults.

- must be able to let clients make their own decisions (within reason) and learn from their mistakes.

- must be good role models. ("Pay no attention to the man behind the curtain. Do as I say, not as I do!")

- must be task-oriented and able to teach goal setting and attainment.

- must have a thorough knowledge of normal and abnormal adolescent in order not to over- or under-react to client situations.

- must have good crisis counseling skills.

- must be able to get organized and keep track of hundreds of details.

- must be able to anticipate problems and be sensitive to unexpressed needs of clients.

- must have a good sense of humor and not assume too much responsibility for client mistakes and failures.

"What do you mean he's 17 and living in his own apartment?" asked the judge.

"Your honor, he only has six months of system support left," said the social worker.

"Are you people crazy or just cruel? I would never do that to my own son," replied the judge.

"But your honor, our client will be totally on his own in six months, whether or not he's ready. They say there just isn't enough money to support older teens in this state," said the social worker.

"I can't imagine my son being on his own. He's 24 and hasn't any intentions of paying his own bills. Maybe when he finishes college he'll move out," the judge wondered.

"That's the point, your honor. Youth from 'normal' families are staying at home until their mid-20s and we expect these kids, without the benefit of a caring family to back them up, to be ready at 18. That's why we are starting youth in custody in self-sufficiency classes at 16 and trying to give them at least six months experience living on their own so they have a chance at surviving after they leave care."

"Just when do you hold these classes and what is the age limit?" asked the judge.

"Hello, Independent Living, I'm Mr. Greenjeans, the landlord over at Buckeye Apartments. We have one of your clients, Jon E. Rotten, living in Apartment 3G, and it's not going well at all. I received four calls this weekend from other tenants in the building about loud music (one of our elderly tenant's false teeth fell out because of your client's eight-foot super-woofer), lots of traffic, and disrespectful visitors. The tenants are all gonna move out if this continues. I gave him two warnings myself, but he's not processing right now. I know you all signed a 12-month lease but he's got to go, ASAP!"

"We're sorry for the trouble, Mr. Greenjeans. As we discussed when we moved him in, we never know how a youth will handle the freedom and responsibility of living alone for the first time. I thought he would do better than this. You have been more than patient. We'll go over today and move him out. We'll also make sure the place is cleaned up."

"Do you have anyone else that you want to move in there?"

"Well, yes, we do as a matter of fact."

17
Special Populations

"When I ran a boys' group home, we were forever sign-ing charges on kids who were assaulting other kids or staff or were stealing something from another resident. They knew our staff by name at detention. In our ILP, we rarely sign charges; kids don't seem to start as many fights when there's no one around to break them up. They don't seem to steal from people they don't know and they don't usually run away from their own apartments."

No program model works for everyone. One of the trends in IL is to design programs around the needs of individual youth, not creating a "one size fits all" program. In the child welfare system, the exception is often the rule and programs must be flexible enough to work with a wide range of clients with complex and sometimes multiple problems. This chapter briefly outlines special client populations that require extra attention and/or services. If you ask around, you will find at least one program that has experience with all of these special needs youth.

Teen Mothers

Teen mothers can do well in less restrictive living arrangements. Of-ten, the birth of a child helps the mom focus more on adult priorities and less on adolescent experimentation. Usually the mother will have to show evidence of being able to provide for her child without con-stant supervision. Teen moms should be required to attend parenting classes, sometimes in-home, and should be held to high cleanliness standards. Some programs receive a higher per diem for teen moms and increase face-to-face contact with the mom.

Chemically Dependent Youth

Sometimes ILP staff are the first care providers to correctly diagnose a youth as being chemically dependent. Most established ILPs consider chemically dependent youth at high-risk to fail a program. Many, if not all, chemically dependent youth relapse during the year following treatment.

The opportunity for obtaining drugs and alcohol is high in even the best homes, schools, and neighborhoods. Youth in scattered-site apartments will have daily opportunities to use drugs/alcohol without adults around. Some programs have youth sign contracts that spell out behavioral expectations (e.g., daily AA meetings, regular drugs screens) and the consequences of not following the contract, such as a move to a more restrictive setting or a tightened curfew.

It is wise to have backup plans for these youth in place from the start, as the odds are high that problems will arise.

Youth with Developmental Disabilities

There are a significant number of youth in the child welfare system with undiagnosed developmental disabilities. These youth can be served in all of the models described above, but will need extra attention and services from staff. The first step is to utilize a screening tool to flag any possible disabilities and then to have a thorough assessment completed. Once the problem(s) is clarified, specialized services can help the youth. Clearly, knowing the youth's strengths and limitations and adjusting services accordingly can lead to better outcomes. Many of these clients will need to be linked to adult-system care providers prior to discharge from the child welfare system.

Youth with Long-Term Medical Problems

Youth with a wide range of medical problems can do well in any IL arrangement. Youth with diabetes, sickle cell anemia, seizure disorders, AIDS, severe asthma, and other long-term problems will be referred to ILPs. The choice of living arrangement option depends on their ability to self-manage the problem. Some programs start these clients in supervised settings until they prove to be capable in monitoring medication supply and usage and keeping doctor's appointments.

Youth with Mental Health Issues

Studies indicate that a high percentage of foster youth have a diagnosable mental health disorder. Many of these youth can be served in any of the models described above. An ILP needs to assess the severity of the problem, the frequency and nature of symptoms, and level of support needed by the youth before any placement choice is made. Youth on medication are almost always placed in supervised settings but can live alone if responsible and more frequently supervised. Consultation with mental health professionals and/or psychiatrists is essential.

Youth with Physical Disabilities

Youth with significant physical disabilities are usually involved with a more specialized service system, or should be connected with such services.

Sex Offenders

Juvenile sex offenders eventually move back to their communities, with or without supervision. Many of these youth are repeating abusive behaviors perpetrated upon them, and with treatment no longer offend. Often the abuse happened only within the family and never involved anyone outside of the family. ILPs may be asked to consider accepting a sex offender who cannot return home due to the victim's presence. Programs that accept these clients use electronic monitoring, enforced curfews, daily visits, mandatory sex offender individual/group therapy, and weekly meetings with probation or parole officers. Clients who show signs of re-offending or contract noncompliance are quickly moved to more restrictive settings or re-incarcerated. There are assessments available to determine the risk of re-offending.

Youth with Criminal Histories

These youth are often among the most difficult clients. Youth with deep-rooted character disorders make it difficult to establish the trust needed for an ILP to place them in a less restrictive setting. At the same time, keeping these clients in supervised groups settings can create problems for other clients and general order-keeping. A referring agency might downplay such a youth's negative behaviors to get him/ her out of an institution. A youth's exemplary institutional behavior might not last a day when out on his own.

ILP staff must learn to recognize signs that a client might be up to criminal activities such as drug dealing or harboring runaways or stolen goods. A combination of electronic monitoring, frequent random visits, regular meetings with parole officers, drug screens, and strict expectations needs to be in place for this group to be in an unsupervised setting. Often the alternative is for the youth to be released without any supervision or monitoring at all.

Hygienically Impaired Clients

Not to be facetious, but there certain clients whose main issue in an ILP is poor hygiene. Youth growing up with neglectful parents or in extreme poverty might have low expectations for personal hygiene and apartment cleanliness. ILPs renting from private landlords will have to address this situation or risk losing a landlord willing to rent to future teens. These youth might need to be shown in detail how to thoroughly clean an apartment with frequent visits made to confront any lapse.

Some programs give a youth a deadline by which to have cleaned his/her site, after which part of their allowance or savings is given to someone else to clean it for the client. Most messy clients hate the idea of a stranger sifting through their stuff.

Youth Involved in Gangs

Youth without stable families are vulnerable to becoming involved in a gang. Gang leaders target such youth, as they know they are in need of a sense of belonging and perceived protection. Some youth come to ILPs wanting to get away from a gang or want to move to another area where gangs are not an issue. Some youth fit the "wannabe" profile and, in spite of what they say or show you, are not really involved in gangs. Others are certified members and will need to be told of the program's position on gang involvement. Some programs have visitor limitations that set curfews on visitors and limit the number allowed to visit. A youth whose living arrangement becomes a focus of gang activities might have to be relocated to a more supervised setting.

Part III, The Future of Independent Living Programs, examines how we evaluation the successes of such programs—and what these successes mean for the future of ILPs.

Part III: The Future of Independent Living Programs

18
Defining Success

"Carl stopped by yesterday. He looked great and seems to have grown out of his Tasmanian Devil phase. I know his old landlord will never rent to us again! Î never thought he'd make it after we kicked him out. But now, he's got a full-time job, a car, a girlfriend, and he wants to come in and talk to the kids in the program now. He thinks he can convince them to not do all of the crazy stuff he did."

Research on ILP outcomes is slowly developing (see suggested readings in Appendix A). Most programs being developed are based on community need or the success of other programs. It may be many years before the IL field can develop programs based on hard research. Keep in mind that a study might find results that do not match the observations of your program. A study looking at youth from a state with few advanced IL services in place might not find the positive outcomes that you have in your community. Until then, it may be helpful to share the observations of program directors who have been running ILPs for a while.

A demand for increased accountability, however, is compelling IL programs to develop outcome measures and define success. This is where it gets interesting. If virtually no families are turning out completely self-sufficient 18-year-olds, then it is almost statistically impossible for IL programs to do so. The age 18 no longer has the developmental significance that it had in the old days when youth were married and working full-time jobs at age 18 or 20. Thus, releasing a fully self-sufficient 18-year-old from a severely dysfunctional family is more a miracle than a success. But, this is not to say that it doesn't happen frequently in ILPs around the country.

What outsiders (referring agencies, courts, the public) consider success and what you consider success can be extremely different. What the youth considers success might be called a negative discharge by someone else. Here are some examples that demonstrate the difficulty of defining success in an ILP

Example #1

Joe was in the ILP for three months. He did little while in the program, but he did complete life skills training and asked a lot of questions. When he was terminated, he went to stay with a 19-year-old friend. Joe had no job, no money saved, and no GED. Six months later, he came by the office to see his former social worker. He looked great, had a full-time job working nights in a factory, and had his own place. "It took me a while, but I finally got it together."

Example #2

Sheila graduated from high school and saved $1,000 while in the ILP. She left care with a fully furnished apartment and a full-time job. Three months later she came to the ILP office and said she was homeless. Her mom had moved in with her and, due to her crack habit, cleaned her out in a few weeks.

Example #3

Jeff never did well in any placement. He was kicked out of three group homes and was removed from five foster homes. He spent a total of 55 days in detention before his seventeenth birthday, due to more than 25 various charges. The ILP took him in because no one else in town would even return the caseworker's phone calls. Jeff spent his last six months in custody living in his own apartment. He worked occasionally, but didn't put any effort into his GED program. There were no criminal charges during his ILP stay.

Example # 4

Ayesha spent her last four years in a foster home. She was afraid of leaving her foster home and seemed anxious about living alone. Her mom was deceased and she never met her father. However, she did great in the ILP, obtained her GED, and held a job at Wendy's for six months straight. A month before her eighteenth birthday, she told her ILP social worker she was pregnant and was leaving the program to live with her boyfriend.

Example #5

Kim did poorly in the ILP. If there was a choice between two evils, she chose both. ILP staff spent hours going over with her the results of her actions, which included getting evicted from two separate apartments. She seemed to have a genetic predisposition toward chaos and finally ran away from her own fully furnished apartment with all of her bills paid, leaving many of her possessions behind. A year later she came to the ILP office and told staff how well she was doing. "I'm completely self-sufficient now. I love my job and share an apartment with a friend from work. You taught me a lot, but I had to run wild for a while."

Example #6

Jack spent a year in his ILP's supervised apartment program. The staff of the ILP did a thorough assessment of Jack's abilities and concluded that he was mildly mentally retarded and had numerous learning disabilities. Jack did well when his single mom was alive, but when she died, he went into a tailspin. The ILP helped Jack get a job through the Bureau of Vocational Rehabilitation and found a volunteer to work one-on-one with Jack to get him through a life skills program. But everyone knew that Jack would never be able to live totally on his own. The ILP connected Jack with an adult group home. Jack might need a similar type of living arrangement for the rest of his life. He would never pass a GED, even with daily individual tutoring, and he never seemed to understand the budgeting process.

As you can see, "success" isn't always immediate. Some of the youth in the above examples really did benefit from IL services, but not immediately. If we were to pull a random group of 17-year-olds from a local high school and put them in their own apartment for six to nine months and then told them they were on their own, would they fare any better than child welfare youth? Some would say that child welfare youth would do better, because they already had experience living without quality adult support.

Independent Living Programs are using various assessment tools, some purchased and some created in-house, to measure success. These can be useful to determine areas of needed improvement and gaps in knowledge. Programs are finding, however, that there is not necessarily a correlation between how well a youth does on an assessment and how well s/he performs when living independently. It is important for any assessment to measure behavioral components, as well as acquisition of knowledge.

Success also must be defined in terms of the potential of the youth and the amount of time an ILP has available to work with her or him. Some youth will never be able pass a GED test. Given an unrealistically short time frame, some youth would be better off looking for a full-time job than to spend their last six months in the system in high school with two years left before they could graduate. In this case, looking at graduation rates as a measure of success would miss the point.

Goals must be individualized and take into account the youth's previous level of functioning, mental health issues, time left in the system, the youth's hopes and dreams, the community's expectations, the level of possible staff involvement, the local economy, the cost of housing, and other factors.

The difficulty in keeping track of youth exiting the system for a period of time after discharge will always make it hard to measure the long-term impact of ILP efforts.

TABLE 6: The Independent Living Success
Formula

$$S = \frac{\$ + CE}{SD} \times \frac{CP}{CR} \times \frac{SE}{Xf} + T$$

S   = Client Success
$ = Funding: Ya gotta have it!
CE = Client Effort: The most important variable.
SD = System Disorganization: This can undermine client motivation
        and even the most substantial funding.
CP = Client Potential: The more the better, but limited youth with
        motivation do better than gifted youth with no motivation.
CR = Client Resistance: This can undermine potential.
Xf = Unknowns (X factors).
SE = Staff Effort.
T   = Time: The more the better. Next to CE, could be the most im-
        portant variable. (However, sometimes a limited time can force
        quick changes.)

(Math majors—please contact me if this isn't mathematically correct!)

Defining Success: One Client at a Time*

In all fields of social services, providers are being asked to show the results of their efforts. Funding decreases and competition between child welfare care providers have lead to calls for increased accountability. As most ILP staffers know, defining success in the field of independent living is complicated.

One is tempted to take the easy way out and quote some beefy sounding number: "Oh, we have about an 86% success rate." But to anyone who knows teens and the world of Independent Living, that answer would be correctly labeled meaningless or simply not good enough.

---

* This section is reprinted (with minor changes) with permission of Daily Living. Defining success: One client at a time. (1993, Fall). *Daily Living, 7*, 8, 12.

Attainment of the original goal of the Independent Living movement, to prepare young adults in out-of-home care for responsible adult living, finds itself against a rising tide of unemployment and housing problems where even college-educated adults are struggling.

If most Americans stay at home or return home after moving out and failing to remain self-sufficient, what does this mean for a field that is attempting to turn out self-sufficient adults at 18 without the possibility of ongoing family support?

Usually, the general public wants to see numbers related to such measures as:

- diplomas/ GED completed

- months of employment and money saved

- the number of youth who leave the system completely, i.e., not on welfare

- clients competing a life skills training program

- clients getting into college or the Armed Services

But the significant abstract gains of individuals sometimes are more indicative of client and program success.

What are the significant life changes that can happen to a youth with the support of an ILP? Some of these changes are not the kind that would show up on most evaluations or measures of success. For example, we feel that a client succeeds when she or he:

- joins a group of positive peers for the first time.

- becomes more assertive with negative peers and family members.

- distances him/herself from abusive people.

- is able to let go of unrealistic fantasies about family support.

- learns how to feel comfortable around members of another race or gender.

- has no problems in an apartment situation for a long period of time.

- seems to enjoy living alone and making daily decisions.

- finds a better living arrangement than we have to offer.

- starts to talk about what *he* or *she* is going to do about a problem.

- no longer has the time to call us on a daily basis with complaints, due to being so busy with daily tasks.

- shows improved insight into his/her responsibility for creating problems.

- is able to delay gratification and work toward planned goals.

- influences other teens to ask to participate in IL training.

- establishes healthier boundaries with unstable family members.

- shifts from and external to an internal locus of control.

As the field of Independent Living is researched, some way of measuring these and other significant changes will hopefully be included. Recognizing, reinforcing, and celebrating the intangible successes of individual clients can serve as a foundation for program development. Sharing these observations with other members of the system (i.e., caseworkers, court personnel, foster parents, guardians ad litem, etc.), is an important element in sustaining program support.

Other Indicators of Success in Independent Living Programs (some more measurable than others)

- Left system with potential long-term living arrangement

- Never needs outside financial assistance again

- Increased score on written IL Information Test

- Increased score on Behavioral Checklist

- Improved communication with adult world

- Better awareness of family strengths and limitations

- More independent—takes more responsibility for life situation

- Is more assertive/less passive

- Decrease in delinquent behavior

- Achieved part of an educational goal

- Gained work experience

- Improved mental health/no further need for education

- Group attendance/participation improved

- Better able to express feelings and ask for help

- Responded to therapy

- Knows that s/he *can't* make it alone

Improvement in any one of these areas indicates some success. Failure to improve in any one of these areas could undo success in others. Attempts to simplify outcome measurements usually result in discussions about numerous other factors involved in the client's life situation that need to be considered. The important debate about what constitutes success in IL programs will probably never end, but dedicated people will learn a lot about how to improve IL services in the process.

19
Is It All Worth It?

 "Tenesha, you can't baby-sit your cousin's quints over here. We can't accept the liability and their strollers are blocking Mr. Trump's access to his apartment."

Each community must decide just how far it will go to assist youth who are unable to live with their families upon discharge from care. Certainly, the easiest thing to do is to take the "we're not responsible for anyone after 18" approach. The age 18 dividing line between the juvenile and adult systems is essentially meaningless in developmental terms, if most youth are being supported by parents until their mid-20s.

Most conscientious child welfare agencies feel that their responsibility for a youth's well-being extends into a future beyond age 18. Some foundations (e.g., The Casey Family Program) already assume this responsibility. Administrators and community leaders who feel that youth today ought to be able to be self-sufficient at 18, as they were, need to be made aware of the differences between then and now that make it much harder to become fully self-sufficient.

Independent Living services are often seen as an optional, extra service to many communities. These services need to be integrated into the child welfare system and seen as important as family preservation and reunification components. For thousands of youth nationwide, the ability to obtain long-term support from any family, be it biological, foster, or adoptive, is not going to be there on a consistent basis.

The survival of these youth depends on the ability to function and live independently in the community.

There is no doubt that a lot of risk is involved in placing a youth in an individual apartment or other, less restrictive setting. There are infinite headaches involved with creating and operating group living situations. But a system designed for ease of operation instead of meeting the needs of the youth in its care will be ineffective in fulfilling its mission: to meet the needs of our children and young adults.

Appendix A
Independent Living Resources

Organizations

Ansell and Associates
(*Daily Living*, the national IL magazine; IL resources; training and consulting)
3837 Northdale, #176
Tampa, FL 33624
813/264-1057
FAX: 813/265-0446
E-mail dansell@kcii.com
http://www.youthlifeskills.com

At-Risk Resources
(catalog of resources for at-risk youth)
135 Dupont Street
P.O. Box 760
Plainville, NY 11803-0760
800/99-YOUTH
FAX: 516/349-5521
http://www.at-risk.com

Boys Town Press
(catalog of resources for youth-serving professionals)
14100 Crawford St.
Boys Town, NE 68010
800/282-6657

Child First, Inc.
(training resources catalog)
P.O. Box 49156
Jacksonville Beach, FL 32240-9156
904/249-3799
FAX: 904/249-3799
E-mail: child1st@tu.infi.net

Child Welfare League of America
(training and consulting, resource catalog)
440 First Street NW, Third Floor
Washington, DC 20001-2085
202/638-2952
FAX: 202/638-4004
http://www.cwla.org

Daniel Memorial Institute
(IL conferences, training, and resources catalog)
4203 Southpoint Boulevard
Jacksonville, FL 32216
800/226-7612
FAX: 904/296-1953
E-mail: DanielKids@aol.com
http://www.danielmemorial.org

Independent Living Resources
(IL resources catalog, training, and consulting)
4324 Thetford Road
Durham, NC 27707-5700
919/402-0262
800/820-0001
FAX: 919/419-1651
E-mail: ilrinc@mindspring.com

Janus Book Publishers
(catalog of resources)
2501 Industrial Parkway West
Hayward CA, 94545
800/227-2395

Kids Rights (catalog of resources)
10100 Park Cedar Drive
Charlotte, NC 28210
800/892-KIDS
FAX: 704/541-0113

Lighthouse Youth Services, Inc.
(IL resources)
1527 Madison Rd.
Cincinnati, Ohio
513/475-5680 ext. 200

National Independent Living Association
c/o Cathy Welsh
South Bronx Human Dev. Corp.
Development Organation, Inc.
One Fordham Plaza, Suite 900
Bronx, NY 10458
718/295-5501
FAX: 718/733-2957

National Resource Center for Youth Services
(youth resource catalog, training and consulting, IL conferences)
The University of Oklahoma
202 W. Eighth Street
Tulsa, OK 74119-1419
918/585-2986
FAX: 918/592-1841
E-mail: rbaker@ou.edu
http://www.nrcys.ou.edu

Northwest Media
(IL-focused resources, videos, books)
326 West 12th Avenue
Eugene, Oregon 97401
800/777-6636
FAX: 541/343-0177

School-to-Work
(resource catalog)
P.O. Box 9
Calhoun, KY 42327-0009
800/962-6662

South Bronx Human Dev. Corp.
(IL resource library)
Development Organation, Inc.
One Fordham Plaza, Suite 900
Bronx, NY 10458
718/295-5501
FAX: 718/733-2957

Sunburst Communications
(adolescent resources catalog)
101 Castleton Street
Pleasantville, NY 10570
800/431-1934
FAX: 914/747-4109

Wisconsin Clearinghouse for Prevention Resources
(resource catalog)
University Health Services
University of Wisconsin-Madison
Dept. 7B
P.O. Box 1468
Madison, WI 53701-1468
800/322-1468
FAX: 608/262-6346

People with Independent Living Housing or Related Field Experience

Dottie Ansell
3837 Northdale, #176
Tampa, FL 33624
813/264-1057
FAX: 813/265-0446
E-mail: dansell@kcii.com
http://www.youthlifeskills.com

Kathy Crowe
Adolescent Consulting Services
86 Sefton Drive
Edgewood, RI 02905
401/461-5406
FAX: 401/461-5406
E-mail: kcrowe@aol.com

Bill Griffin
Brendan Resources
4324 Thetford
Durham, NC 27707-5700
919/489-1351

Joan Morse
6945 108th Street
Forest Hills, NY 11375
718/793-2356

Robin Nixon
Child Welfare League of America
440 First Street NW, Third Floor
Washington, DC 20001/2085
202/942-0309
FAX: 202/638-4004
E-mail: rnixon@cwla.org

Bill Pinto
Connecticut Department of
   Children, Youth and Families
500 Hudson
Hartford, CT 06106
860/550-6471

Jackie Smith
Spectrum Youth and Family
   Services
31 Elmwood
Burlington, VT 05401
802/864-7423 (217)

Dianne Stevens
Director, Emancipation Services
Franklin County Children's
   Services
1951 Gantz Road
Grove City, OH 43123
614/275-2586

Byron Wright
Kenosha Human Development
   Services
5407 8th Avenue
Kenosha, WI 53140
414/657-7188

Suggested Readings

Allen, M., Bonner, K., & Greenan, L. (1988). Federal legislative support for independent living. *Child Welfare, 67* (6), 515-527.

Barth, R. P. (1990). On their own: The experiences of youth after foster care. *Child and Adolescent Social Work, 7* (5), 419-440.

Barth, R. P. (1986, May/June). Emancipation services for children in foster care. *Social Work,* 165-171.

Brinkman, A. S., Dey, S., & Cuthbert, P. (1991). A supervised independent-living orientation program for adolescents. *Child Welfare, 70* (1), 69-80.

Cook, R. (1994). Are we helping foster care youth prepare for their future? Special issue: Preparing foster youth for adulthood. *Children and Youth Services Review, 16* (3-4), 213-229.

Cook, R. (1991). *A national evaluation of Title IV-E foster care independent living programs for youth. Phase 2: Final report.* Rockville, MD: Westat, Inc.

Cook, R. (1988). Trends and needs in programming for independent living. *Child Welfare, 67* (6), 497-514.

Courtney, M. E., & Barth, R. P. (1996). Pathways of older adolescents out of foster care: Implications for independent living services. *Social Work, 41* (1), 75-83.

Courtney, M. E., Piliavin, I., & Grogan-Taylor, A. (1995). *The Wisconsin study of youth aging out of out-of-home care: A portrait of children about to leave care.* Madison, WI: Institute for Research on Poverty. Available at http://polyglot.1ss.wisc.edu/socwork/foster/.

English, D. J., Kouidou-Giles, S., & Plocke, M. (1994). Readiness for independence: A study of youth in foster care. Special issue: Preparing foster youth for adulthood. *Children and Youth Services Review, 16* (3-4), 147-158.

Festinger, T. (1983). *No one ever asked us ... A postscript to foster care.* New York: Columbia University Press.

Hahn, A. (1994). The use of assessment procedures in foster care to evaluate readiness for independent living. Special issue: Preparing foster youth for adulthood. *Children and Youth Services Review, 16* (3-4), 171-179.

Hardin, M. (1988). New legal options to prepare adolescents for independent living. *Child Welfare, 67* (6), 529-545.

Iglehart, A. P. (1994). Adolescents in foster care: Predicting readiness for independent living. Special issue: Preparing foster youth for adulthood. *Children and Youth Services Review, 16* (3-4), 159-169.

Kroner, M. J. (1988). Living arrangement options for young people preparing for independent living. *Child Welfare, 67* (6), 547-562.

Lammert, M., & Timberlake, E.M. (1986). Termination of foster care for the older adolescent: Issues of emancipation and individuation. *Child and Adolescent Social Work, 3* (1), 26-37.

Mallon, G. (1992). Junior life skills: An innovation for latency age children in out-of-home care. *Child Welfare, 71* (6), 585-591.

Mech, E. V. (1988). Introduction. Preparing foster adolescents for self-support: A new challenge for child welfare services. *Child Welfare, 67* (6), 487-495.

Mech, E. V. (1994). Foster youths in transition: Research perspectives on preparation for independent living. *Child Welfare, 73* (5), 603-623.

Mech, E. V., & Leonard, E. L. (1988). Volunteers as resources in preparing foster adolescents for self-sufficiency. *Child Welfare, 67* (6), 595-607.

Mech, E. V., Ludy-Dobson, C., & Hulseman, F. (1994). Life skills knowledge: A survey of foster adolescents in three placement settings. Special issue: Preparing foster youth for adulthood. *Children and Youth Services Review, 16* (3-4), 181-200.

Mech, E. V., & Rycraft, J. R. (1994). *Preparing foster youths for adult living: Proceedings of an invitational research conference.* Washington, DC: Child Welfare League of America.

Modrcin, M. J. (1989). Emotionally handicapped youth in transition: Issues and principles for program development. *Community Mental Health Journal, 25* (3), 219-227.

Ryan, P., McFadden, E. J., Rice, D., & Warren, B. L. (1988). The role of foster parents in helping youth people develop emancipation skills. *Child Welfare, 67* (6), 563-572.

Stone, H. D. (1987). *Ready set go: An agency guide to independent living.* Washington, DC: Child Welfare League of America.

Tatara, T., Casey, P., Nazar, K., Richmond, F., Diethorn, R., & Chapmond, T. (1988). Evaluation of independent-living programs. *Child Welfare, 67* (6), 609-624.

Waldinger, G., & Furman, W. M. (1994). Two models of preparing foster youths for emancipation. Special issue: Preparing foster youth for adulthood. *Children and Youth Services Review, 16* (3-4), 201-212.

Westat, Inc. (1988). *A national evaluation of Title IV-E foster care independent living programs for youth. Final report.* Washington, DC: U. S. Department of Health and Human Services.

Appendix B
Helpful Forms

This appendix contains forms that might be helpful in your work. The size has been minimized to save space. You will probably need to customize these forms for your client, program, and community relatives.

Helpful Form #1   Weekly Independent Living Awareness
                   Checklist
Helpful Form #2   Sample Intake and Orientation Checklist
Helpful Form #3   General Expectations of Client
Helpful Form #4   Weekly Client Monitoring Checklist
Helpful Form #5   A Sample Rules Agreement Form
Helpful Form #6   Red Flag Policy for High-Risk Clients
Helpful Form #7   Personal Safety Agreement Form
Helpful Form #8   Termination Checklist
Helpful Form #9   Sample Criteria for Acceptance into an
                   Individual Apartment Program
Helpful Form #10   A Sample Host Home Contract

Helpful Form #1:
Weekly Independent Living Awareness Checklist

(To be filled out by client weekly until all information is automatic.)

Name _____ Date _____

Address _____

City _____ State _____ ZIP _____

Phone number _____ Social Security number _____

School grade _____

Caseworker _____ Phone number _____

Place of employment _____

Landlord's name _____

Monthly rent $ _____ Due date for rent _____
Monthly utility bill $ _____ Due date _____
Monthly phone bill $ _____ Due date _____
How much money did you earn this week? $_____
How much money did you receive from someone else this week? $ _____
From the independent living program? $ _____ From TANF? $ _____
From food stamps? $ _____ From other sources? $ _____
When will you turn 18? _____
How much money do you have saved? $ _____
How much did you take out of your savings this week? $ _____
What did you buy? _____
How many days did you attend school last week? _____
How many days were you tardy? _____
What subjects need work? _____
Who paid your rent for this month? _____
Who paid your utility bill? _____
Who paid your phone bill? _____
Who gave you food for money? _____

Do you have your state ID card with you? _____

During the past week, did you do any of the following?

- ❑ shop for groceries
- ❑ take care of transportation
- ❑ do dishes
- ❑ do your laundry
- ❑ change light bulbs
- ❑ clean kitchen floor
- ❑ cook your own meals

- ❑ wake yourself up in the morning
- ❑ clean your bathroom
- ❑ take out garbage
- ❑ sweep all floors
- ❑ straighten up apartment
- ❑ complete homework

How many life skills chapters have you completed? _____

Which one did you complete last week? _____

What other activities did you do to help take care of yourself last week? _____

_____

What are some things that others did to help you last week? _____

_____

What are you planning to do this week to improve your situation? _____

_____

Did you make any appointments this week? _____   If yes, which ones? _____

Did you miss any appointments? _____   Which one? _____

When was your last dental checkup? _____

Who is your dentist? _____

When was your last doctor's appointment? _____

Who is your doctor? _____

What were your biggest problems last week? _____

Is your smoke detector working? _____ Battery OK? _____

What community resources did you use last week? _____

Did you have any family contact last week? _____

Do you have any outstanding debts or unpaid bills? _____

When will you get your next report card? _____

What were your contacts with the independent living program last week? _____

Do you have with you or at your apartment the following:

- ❑ your state ID card
- ❑ a certified copy of your birth certificate
- ❑ an original copy of your social security card

- ❑ a library card
- ❑ a calendar for writing down appointments
- ❑ an emergency phone list

What do you need from the independent living program? _____

_____

Helpful Form #2:
Sample Intake and Orientation Checklist

(Things that need to be done when placing a youth in his/her own apartment.)

Client name: _____ Date: _____

Intake person: _____

- ❏ Social worker assigned to client/client introduced to staff
- ❏ File started
- ❏ Permission to Place Form signed
- ❏ Permission to Provide Medical Treatment Form signed
- ❏ Consent to Release Information Form signed
- ❏ Intake packet completed by referring agency caseworker
- ❏ Directions to office received/office phone number received
- ❏ Apartment procured/landlord met/apartment condition checklist signed
- ❏ Rental information to director
- ❏ Deposit paid/lease signed/copies of lease to director
- ❏ Lease read to client/copy given to client
- ❏ Keys copied/two sets to client/one set to caseworker
- ❏ Telephone service started/phone received by client
- ❏ Phone number entered into computer
- ❏ Utilities started
- ❏ Weekly Independent Living Awareness Form explained
- ❏ Original birth certificate received
- ❏ Original Social Security card received
- ❏ Physical completed or set up/report filed
- ❏ Dental appointment set up
- ❏ Start-Up List completed
- ❏ Client Information Sheet completed/copy to director
- ❏ Basic supplies purchased
- ❏ Rules read and signed
- ❏ Treatment plan completed and signed by client
- ❏ Important phone numbers posted by phone
- ❏ Life skills book received by client/program explained
- ❏ Communication with staff understood/pager tested
- ❏ Policies reviewed and signed by client (project #1)

- ☐ Emergency procedures understood
- ☐ Apartment operations understood: stove, water, thermostat, air conditioner, washer, dryer, etc.
- ☐ Procedures for reporting apartment problems explained
- ☐ Daily call-in understood
- ☐ Budget Form completed
- ☐ Transportation understood/bus schedule received
- ☐ Allowance Agreement Form signed
- ☐ Life Skills Assessment (100?'s) completed and reviewed
- ☐ Letter sent to school counselor
- ☐ Apartment Cleaning Checklist Form reviewed and posted
- ☐ _____
- ☐ _____
- ☐ _____

Completed on _____

Helpful Form #3:
General Expectations of Client

(To be reviewed with client moving into her/his own place.)

To help things work well for both you and our staff, we ask that each client follow the guidelines below.

1. Inform your caseworker or the director immediately of any emergencies, including medical problems, legal problems, damage to your apartment, school suspensions, trouble at work, and trouble in the neighborhood. If you are in any type of trouble, do not hesitate to call. Do not attempt to cover up any wrongdoing. We are here to HELP you.

2. Learn the program rules and policies and follow them. You should not need "warnings" at this stage.

3. Never leave your phone off the hook. We will be making routine calls to make sure you are doing well.

4. Call us whenever you are
   - not going to school or work
   - not able to make it to group
   - not able to keep an appointment
   - going to be late for an appointment with independent living program staff
   - not going to be at your apartment by curfew

5. Always think of your personal safety. Never put yourself in a position that could be dangerous. Learn and follow the program guidelines for personal safety.

6. Remember that you are a representative of our program. Whatever you do will be a reflection of the entire independent living program. Our staff is proud of the program, and we want you to be proud as well.

7. We want to hear from you daily during the week. Call during your lunch break from school to let us know how things are going.

8. Please be aware that our staff have many responsibilities and their time is valuable and often prescheduled. If you arrange a meeting time with your social worker or program director, be sure that you are on time. If you're going to be late, call. Don't expect your social worker to always be available the moment that you call her or him. S/he will be acting according to the importance of each task.

9. Always show respect for your landlord, your resident manager, and the other tenants. Learn to become more aware of how your actions affect others.

Helpful Form #4:
Weekly Client Monitoring Checklist

(To be kept in client file to document service delivery.)

Client name _____

Months in program _____ Planned termination date _____

Last contacts _____

Interventions _____

Smoke detector OK _____ Stove OK _____

Apartment condition _____

Furniture needed _____

Repairs needed _____

Health _____

School attendance _____

School progress _____

Work situation _____

Savings ($) _____ Life skills completed to date _____

Major problems _____

Incidents _____

Comments _____

Things to be done _____

Social worker signature _____ Date _____

Helpful Form #5:
A Sample Rules Agreement Form

(To be read and signed by client at entry into program.)

The Independent Living Program is designed to give you an opportunity to learn how to live on your own and become a responsible adult member of the community. As a member of the program, you must agree to the following rules.

1. You must be involved in a productive activity like school or work for at least 20 hours a week. If you are not enrolled in school, you might be required to attend temporary classes at the shelter or come to the Independent Living Program office daily until you are enrolled. If you are not working, you might be required to come to the office daily until you are employed.

2. You must spend each night in your apartment and may not have overnight visitors unless approved in advance by Independent Living Program staff. You are required to be at your apartment by 11 P.M. on weekdays and 1 A.M. on weekends. Visitors leave by 11 P.M.

3. It is your responsibility to keep your apartment clean and in good condition. You are responsible for everything that happens in your apartment, including the behavior of your visitors. You may not have more than two visitors at a time in the apartment. Using or possessing drugs or alcohol is never allowed in the apartment. **Remember, the lease belongs to the program and not to you.** You will be responsible for paying for any damages.

4. You will receive an allowance of up to $60 weekly to be used for food, transportation, and supplies only; $15 of this amount will be saved weekly and will be available to you when you leave the program. If you are working, this amount will be kept in a savings account until you leave the program. If you lose your allowance, you will not receive another check.

5. You are expected to call the office daily (during the week) to report on your well-being and daily progress. You are also required to meet with your program social worker twice a week or as scheduled.

6. You are also expected to actively work toward completing the life skills training program, which consists of 24 self-guided projects. You will receive $25 for each completed project, which be given to you in four monthly installations after you successfully complete the program.

Refusal to cooperate with the program rules and/or staff can result in termination from the program. **Involvement in any type of illegal activity is grounds for immediate termination.**

I have read and understand the above rules. I agree to follow them at all times.

_____

Client   Date

_____

Staff   Date

Helpful Form #6:
Red Flag Policy for High-Risk Clients

There will be times when a client referred to an Independent Living Program by the correctional system needs more intensive supervision or possibly incarceration. A client's behavior can suddenly change, even after a period of responsibility. This could be the result of alcohol or chemical dependency issues, or a re-involvement in criminal activities.

The parole/probation officer and the Independent Living Program (ILP) social worker have different perspectives on a client's behavior. The parole/probation officer knows more about the client's past record and baseline behavior. The ILP worker knows more about the present behavior of the client. Either one might feel that some action needs to be taken to confront the client about negative behaviors or the need to take more serious disciplinary action.

A client can be given "red flag" status by either correctional system staff or ILP staff when

1. the client is AWOL for more than 24 to 36 hours
2. the client is possibly involved in criminal activity
3. the client misses a meeting with his/her parole officer
4. the client becomes involved with known criminals
5. a client who is a sex offender misses a treatment meeting
6. a client has alcohol or drugs in her/his apartment
7. any other situation in which staff feel that something is going wrong

If a client is "red flagged," the following should happen:
1. Both the correctional system (CS) supervisor and the ILP director should be notified of the situation.
2. The CS supervisor and the ILP staff member should have daily phone contact, by voice mail if necessary, to discuss his/her observation of the client's behavior.
3. The ILP worker will have daily contact with the client by phone and will visit the client's apartment at least three times weekly.
4. A meeting with the client, CS staff, the ILP worker, and the ILP director will be held at either office to write up a behaviorally specific contract the client will need to follow.
5. The client will be held accountable to the contract and possibly by terminated from the program or re-incarcerated if he/she fails to follow the contract.

The "red flag" status can be lifted only when both CS staff and ILP staff agree that it is OK to do so.

Helpful Form #7:
Personal Safety Agreement Form

(To be read and signed by client at program orientation.)

In the interest of your personal safety and well-being, we ask you to review and follow the guidelines written below.

1. Never allow a stranger into your apartment. Never let a stranger know where you live.
2. Make sure you know and trust someone well enough before you give them your phone number.
3. Hitchhiking is not allowed while in the program.
4. Report to your Independent Living Program social worker and/or landlord whenever you have any problems with gas, electricity, or plumbing in your apartment.
5. Let your ILP social worker and landlord know of any malfunctioning locks.
6. Make sure you have a smoke detector and good batteries in it. Check it on a weekly basis.
7. Before leaving your apartment, make sure
   - your stove is turned off
   - all water faucets are turned off
   - all appliances are turned off (irons, radios, TVs)
   - all windows and doors are locked
8. Make sure you know and trust someone well enough before you get into a car with her/him. Never get into a car with someone who is under the influence of drugs or alcohol.
9. Follow your curfew. Use good judgment when you are out late at night. Make sure you have a ride home from any late night activity. If possible, do not walk alone on the street after 11 P.M.
10. Weapons are a potential danger to you and are not allowed in the program. No guns, knives, brass knuckles, etc., will be tolerated.
11. Be knowledgeable about fire prevention. Know in advance what you would do in case of a fire. Make sure you have been provided with a fire extinguisher and know how to use it.
12. Post on your telephone the numbers of any emergency service.
13. If you do not know how to operate your stove, oven, or other appliances, be sure that you ask for help in learning how to do so.

I have read and understand the above safety guidelines.

Client _____ Date _____

Staff _____ Date _____

Helpful Form #8:
Termination Checklist

(To be completed when client leaves the program from own apartment.)

- ☐ Landlord notified
- ☐ Apartment cleaned/emptied
- ☐ Referring agency caseworker notified
- ☐ Accounting office contacted about client terminating
- ☐ Phone closed out or transferred to client
- ☐ Gas and electricity turned off or transferred
- ☐ Keys returned (from client or keys given to client)
- ☐ Savings account closed
- ☐ Lease signed by client
- ☐ Client's new address in computer
- ☐ Last phone bill received
- ☐ Evaluation returned to director
- ☐ Deposit received or returned
- ☐ Close-Out Form on file
- ☐ Close-Out Form signed by director
- ☐ _____
- ☐ _____
- ☐ _____

Director _____   Date _____

Helpful Form #9:
Sample Criteria for Acceptance into an Individual Apartment Program

1. Client must be between 16 1/2 and 18. (19-year-olds can be accepted under special circumstances.)
2. Client must be a resident of this state.
3. Client must not be actively psychotic.
4. Client must not be able to return home at this point in time.
5. Client must be willing to contract for services and participate in the program.
6. Client must be able to understand the program goals and benefits from the experience of living alone.
7. Client must be sponsored by an organization able to pay program per diem and remain actively involved in the client's life.

Helpful Form #10:
A Sample Host Home Contract

Client: Steve Walters
Agency: Millennium Youth Services
Host: Ruth Smith
Custodial agency: Clinton County Children's Services
Date: _____

Host Home Responsibilities
1. Provide housing and furnishing to Steve until 12/31/99, providing that client meets his contract terms.
2. Have weekly contact with Millennium ILP staff.
3. Alert ILP staff weekly of any concerns, problems, or rule infractions.
4. Have daily contact with Steve, by phone if necessary.
5. Act as a positive role model to resident.

Client Responsibilities
1. Follow all ILP rules and policies.
2. Attend school and call ILP office daily.
3. Follow host home rules and respect host property.
4. Attend weekly therapy groups.
5. Budget weekly allowance money according to agreement.
6. Purchase own food, clothing, and personal items.
7. Call ILP office daily to report activities.

Agency Responsibilities
1. Pay host monthly rent of $350.
2. Reimburse Mrs. Smith for half of basic monthly phone bill.
3. Reimburse 30% of monthly utility bill.
4. Make weekly checks of the home.
5. Document weekly progress.
6. Meet weekly with client at home.
7. Have weekly contact with Mrs. Smith, by phone if necessary.

Referring Agency Responsibilities
1. Provide transportation to weekly group meetings.
2. Cover medical and treatment group expenses.
3. Have monthly contact with Steve to assess his progress.
4. Agree to support Steve until 12/31/99.

Any party can cancel this contract if given 30 days' notice. If necessary, Millennium will provide immediate alternative living arrangements.

Client   Host
_____

County Casework   Director of Millennium ILP
_____

About the Author

Mark J. Kroner, M.S.W., L.S.W., is Director of the Division of Self-Sufficiency Services for Lighthouse Youth Services. He has directed the Independent Living Program for Lighthouse since 1986, and has worked with hundreds of young people exiting the child welfare system.

Mr. Kroner, a licensed social worker, has worked in the field as a social worker, a group home director, a group trainer, and a consultant. He served on the National Independent Living Standards Committee of the Child Welfare League of America and on the Ohio State Independent Living Task Force, and served as President of the Ohio Independent Living Association in 1995-96. In addition, he has published numerous articles and workbooks that focus on self-sufficiency development, as well as the boardgame, "Progress and Setbacks."

Mark speaks extensively around the country on independent living issues and has helped dozens of agencies start and develop scattered-site apartment programs. He received his Master's in Social Work in 1997 from the University of Cincinnati, Ohio.

NEW!

From the Child Welfare League of America

Youth Work Resources, Number 1:
Interactive Youth Work Practice

by Mark A. Krueger

Through essays, practice examples, and a curriculum outline, *Interactive Youth Work Practice* promotes the theory that youth develop in moments and interactions. These moments and interactions are enhanced when workers have the capacity to guide, teach, learn, and be with youth, with sensitivity to their developmental capacities and readiness for growth and the multiple contexts within which interactions take place. Youth work is viewed as a shared journey, workers and youth going through the day, learning and growing together!

To Order: 1998/0-87868-707-6   Stock #7076 $16.95

Write:	CWLA	Call:	800/407-6273
	P.O. Box 2019		301/617-7825
	Annapolis Junction, MD 20701		
e-mail:	cwla@pmds.com	Fax:	301/206-9789

Please specify stock #7076. Bulk discount policy (not for resale): 10-49 copies 10%, 50-99 copies 20%, 100 or more copies 40%. Canadian and foreign orders must be prepaid in U.S. funds. MasterCard/Visa accepted.